MONTH-BY-MONTH
PHONICS
FOR UPPER GRADES
A SECOND CHANCE FOR STRUGGLING READERS AND STUDENTS LEARNING ENGLISH

by

Patricia M. Cunningham

and

Dorothy P. Hall

Project Coordinator
Joyce Kohfeldt
I.E.S.S., Kernersville, NC

Editors
Lynn Ruppard
Louise Vaughn

Illustrator
Gene Shanks

DEDICATION

This book is dedicated to all students for whom learning to read is a struggle and to all teachers who don't "write them off," but rather give them a second chance!

ISBN 0-88724-473-4

TABLE OF CONTENTS

Phonics is the current "hot topic." Everyone is talking about phonics, and everyone has an opinion about what should be taught, and how and when it should be taught. **Phonics *is* an important part of reading instruction, but phonics is not all that matters.** In fact, children who come to school with limited reading experiences and who are taught in a "phonics first, phonics only" approach often get the idea that reading is "sounding out words"! You do have to figure out words, but reading is not figuring out words and "sounding good." Figuring out words is the means to the end of understanding, learning, thinking, and enjoying. **Good readers do know phonics and they use phonics to figure out some words; but good readers also recognize the most frequent words instantly as sight words. They use context to check that what they are reading and the words they have figured out make sense.**

The word *balance* is currently in danger of extinction from overuse, but the concept of balance is and will remain a critically-important idea. To us, balance in reading instruction is like a balanced diet. We eat from the different food groups because each group of foods is important to growth. We decide how much of each group should be included in a balanced diet and these amounts change as people grow older. We do not try to decide which of the different groups is best, nor do we go through phases in which "experts" recommend that we eat only from one group!

To become good readers, students need a balanced reading diet. The different "food groups" of balanced reading instruction are Guided Reading, Self-Selected Reading, Writing, and Working with Words (Cunningham and Allington, 1999).

This book provides month-by-month activities for one-quarter of a well-balanced reading diet— the Working With Words block. When this block is combined with the other essential components—Guided Reading, Self-Selected Reading, and Writing—readers grow and enhance their literacy skills at their optimum rates.

As you begin this book, think about the kind of phonics instruction you will find here. For a long time, the phonics debate centered on whether to teach using a synthetic or analytic approach. Synthetic approaches generally teach readers to go letter-by-letter, assigning a pronunciation to each letter and then blending individual letters together. Analytic approaches teach rules (i.e., when an **e** is added to the end of a word, it makes the preceding vowel long). Brain research, however, suggests that the brain is a pattern detector, not a rule applier, and that, while we look at single letters, we are not assigning them sounds; rather we are looking at clusters of letters and considering the letter patterns we know (Adams, 1990).

By the time students move into the upper grades, they are expected to be able to decode and spell most words. Unfortunately, not all students meet this expectation. The inability to decode and spell hinders them in all their subjects and, until they become fluent with words, they make little progress and indeed fall further and further behind. **This book is intended to help struggling readers—whether they are fourth graders or tenth graders—become fluent decoders and spellers. It also provides activities through which students who are learning English can learn to use our English spelling system. The activities in this book are designed to meet five critical word fluency goals:**

Goal 1: Teach students the correct spelling for high-frequency, often irregularly-spelled words such as **they, friend, could, there, their, they're, right, write,** etc.

Goal 2: Teach students how to decode and spell one- and two-syllable words based on words they already know. Students who can read **Crest**® on the toothpaste tube should be able to decode and spell other rhyming words such as **best, rest, pest, infest,** and **request**.

Goal 3: Teach students that spelling rhyming words is not as easy as decoding them because some rhymes, such as **right/bite; claim/name; toad/code,** have two spelling patterns. The reader has to develop a visual checking system and learn to use a dictionary when he is unsure about which pattern looks right.

Goal 4: Teach students key words containing the major prefixes, suffixes and spelling changes and how to use these to decode, spell, and build meaning for many polysyllabic words.

Goal 5: Teach students to use cross checking while reading and a visual checking system while writing to apply what they are learning as they engage in meaningful reading and writing.

While these five goals are those most commonly needed by upper-grade students who have not yet become fluent with words, not all students will need to work on all five. The following pages provide some ways to determine which goals particular students need to work on.

Learning High–Frequency, Commonly Misspelled Words

Goal One

The best way to determine if students need to work on the high-frequency word goal is to have them do several pages of first draft writing on a topic of interest to them, and then analyze their writing to see what they need (see examples, pages 5 and 6). Students who spell **they** as **t-h-a-y**, spell **said** as **s-e-d**, write **couldn't** without the apostrophe and perhaps missing some letters, and use the wrong **to/too/two** or **right/write** need to relearn these high-frequency words. These students are spelling in the logical way—but unfortunately not the correct way. **Notice that you cannot determine this by giving them a spelling test on these words. When focusing their attention on these words, many upper-grade students can spell them correctly but then turn right around and spell them incorrectly in their writing.** Contrary to popular opinion, this is not obstinacy on their part! **Rather the brain has the remarkable ability to make things "automatic" after having processed them several times. Once something is put in the automatic part of the brain, it is carried out without any conscious thought.**

This automatic-making function of the brain is a wonderful asset when it makes things "automatic right." Once a person has had lots of practice driving, she can shift, put on turn signals, steer, etc., while talking to passengers, listening to the radio, planning dinner, or talking on the phone. **The brain can do many automatic things at a time, but only *one* nonautomatic thing at a time.** When children are just beginning to write, they spell words the logical way—**t-h-a-y, s-e-d, f-r-e-n-d**. Because these words are high-frequency, they write them many times, each time spelling them the logical—but wrong—way. After a certain number of times (it varies from brain to brain), the brain assumes this is the correct spelling and puts the spelling in its automatic compartment! Later, the child learns the correct spellings for **they**, **said**, and **friend** on a spelling list but they are only practiced for a week for the test. The child doesn't get enough practice for the brain to replace the spellings in the automatic compartment. **When a person is writing, the brain's nonautomatic power is on meaning and, except for an occasional new word, the brain's automatic compartment takes care of spelling. When the words in that automatic compartment are correct, this is a marvelous function of the brain; but when they are incorrect, we have the often-demonstrated proof that it is not practice that makes perfect, it is *perfect* practice!** (The solution to this problem is not to stop young children from writing until they learn to spell everything correctly but rather to begin a Word Wall in first grade and put the irregular high-frequency words on it so that they don't become "automatic wrong!")

Students who misspell high-frequency words in their writing need lots of perfect practice. Anyone who has ever tried to change an old habit knows that the brain does not like to take things out of the automatic compartment, throw them away, and put them back in there right! **So, look at the first-draft writing of your students and be guided by what you see. Each month, activities will be suggested for re-automatizing these high-frequency words. On page 7 is a list of the words on which this book focuses. (If there are words on the list that all your students spell correctly in their writing, you should omit those. Likewise, if there are high-frequency words your students are misspelling that are not on the list, include these.)**

Student Writing Samples

Below and on page 6 are actual samples from students in the upper elementary grades. Note the high-frequency words such as *friend*, *which*, *about*, *they*, and *were* that are misspelled by the students. By evaluating students' writing samples at the beginning of the year, you can determine what high-frequency words the students need to work on. As you may note with the samples below, many of the misspelled words are actually spelled in a logical way—but not the right way.

"A Day at the Beach"

One day I want to the beech with my ant and uncle. The whether was warm and wendy. We were the frist peeple on the beech.

I saw my frend Andrew at the beech. He was thare with his sister and brother. It was his sisters brithday. We dug wholes in the sand and then put water in the wholes.

We played volliball. My teem one the game. We whent to the ice cream stor to by ice cream. It was a grate day!

"Runaway Ralph"

The story is about a small mouse named Ralph. He always caused trobble. He always rid on his little motorcycle. The setting was in a house. Characters are Ralph, Chum, Gofer, and Garph.

Beginning – A boy named Garph came to stay at the house. He wasent vary happy.

Middle – The boy went up to his room and he saw the mouse. Ralph was talking to him. He was shoked because he saw a mouse talk.

End – Later on Garph had to go to camp. Ralph was sad so he went to look for him and he found him.

"The Lost World – Jurassic Park"

Ien Malcome's girl freind went to Site B, another iland coverd with dinosaurs like Jurassic Park. So Ien went to surch for her.

Thay found a baby T-Rex with a broken leg so thay helped it but momy and dady T-Rex got angry and tryed to push them off a cliff but thay lived.

Then thay got off the island and went home but they had to survie a T-Rex attack in San Deago. Then the T-Rex left the sity with it's baby on a ship.

*Notice how much better this paper would be if the word "they" was correct.

"Charlie and the Chocolate Factory"

This book is abot a boy and his grafather who find a golden ticket wich alows them to go into Willy Wonka's Chocolate Factory. They wer given a secret test wich Charlie passed and he got to live in the factory forever.

I recamend this book to anyone who likes fun and aventurus books.

The preceding student writing samples were based on these literature selections:
Michael Crichton. *The Lost World—Jurassic Park*. New York: Knopf, 1995.
Beverly Cleary. *Runaway Ralph*. New York: Morrow, 1970.
Roald Dahl. *Charlie and the Chocolate Factory*. New York: Knopf Publishing, 1964.

Ninety Commonly Misspelled Words for Upper–Grade Word Walls

about	except	probably	very
again	excited	really	want
almost	favorite	right	was
also	first	said	wear
always	friends	school	weather
another	getting	something	we're
anyone	have	sometimes	went
are	hole	terrible	were
beautiful	I'm	that's	what
because	into	their	when
before	it's	then	where
buy	its	there	whether
by	knew	they	who
can't	know	they're	whole
could	laugh	thought	with
didn't	let's	threw	won
doesn't	myself	through	won't
don't	new	to	wouldn't
enough	no	too	write
especially	off	trouble	your
everybody	one	two	you're
everyone	our	until	
everything	people	usually	

The "Portable Word Wall" on page 133 shows what your Word Wall should look like at the beginning of the school year (after the August/September high-frequency words have been added.) Likewise, the "Portable Word Wall" on page 141 shows what your Word Wall should look like at the end of the school year (after all of the high-frequency words have been added.) Some teachers may prefer starting with a commercially-prepared Word Wall with all of the high-frequency words already printed (Kohfeldt, Cunningham, Hall, 1998).

Goal Two

Learning One– and Two–Syllable Words That Follow a Pattern, but Are Used Less Frequently

When students are reading and come to a word that is used less frequently, one they may not have encountered before in reading, what do they do? Good readers who first encounter words such as **bode**, **spawn**, **swoop**, **inquest**, and **forlorn** do not hesitate long before coming up with the correct pronunciation. Likewise, when writing, good spellers who need to spell words such as **stress**, **cloak**, or **disgrace** either spell them correctly or in an equally possible way. **Cloak** *could* be spelled **c-l-o-k-e**. It just isn't! **Disgrace** *could* be **d-i-s-g-r-a-s-e**. It just isn't!

One clear indicator of a fluent reader and writer is the ability to decode and spell words never seen or used before. Psychologists, who study how our brains process new stimuli, describe **the brain as a pattern detector.** They explain that **when faced with something new—including new words—the brain does a quick search for similar things** (Caine and Caine, 1991). **For words, these similar things are other words that follow the pattern. The patterns in one- and two-syllable words are the beginning letters, which linguists call "onsets," and the rest of the syllables, called "rimes."** In **stress**, the onset is **str** and the rime is **ess**. For **cloak**, the onset is **cl** and the rime is **oak**. In **disgrace**, the onset for the first syllable is **d** and the rime is **is**; for the second syllable the onset is **gr** and the rime is **ace**.

Psychologists call the division of new words into onsets and rimes a "psychological reality," which in simple terms means, "that's just the way the brain does it!" (Treiman, 1985). Numerous experiments have shown that it is much faster and easier to figure out words in which the onset has been changed but the rime is intact than to change the letters following the vowel. Check this out for yourself by reading across the following two rows of words as fast as you can:

can	ban	Fran	span	Stan	van	tan	bran	than
can	cad	cast	cab	calf	cam	cap	cat	cask

Even though you have seen these words before, it takes you milliseconds longer (which can be measured in an experimental computer response setting) to read the second list because you must keep identifying the rime. In the first list, once you have the rime, you can quickly change the onset.

This finding that the way the brain deals with words is to look for the pattern, and that the pattern is contained in the onset and rime, is critical to understanding why many children who have been taught phonics rules or to sound words out letter-by-letter are not successful decoders. The rules lead you to break the rime apart as you consider what the **e** on the end might be doing or whether or not the **r** might be controlling the vowel. Rules explain some of how our phonics system works, but applying rules is not how the brain figures out new words. In addition to the psychological evidence, there is firsthand evidence from hordes of poor readers who "know the rules but just don't use them."

So, students who are not using patterns to read and spell words would likely have difficulty reading pattern-following but less-frequently used words such as **bode**, **spawn**, **swoop**, **inquest**, and **forlorn**. Likewise, these same students would likely spell words such as **stress**, **cloak**, and **disgrace** in a "put down the sounds you hear" fashion as **s-t-r-e-s**, **c-l-o-k**, and **d-i-s-g-r-a-s**. **Activities designed to help students learn to decode and spell pattern-following words will not teach them any phonics rules. Rather they will learn to decode in a brain-friendly way—using the words they know to decode and spell other words.**

Goal Three

Spelling Words with Two or More Possible Patterns

In English, words with the same rime usually (but not always!) rhyme. The complication is that some rhymes have two or three different rimes. This is not a problem when a reader is decoding an unfamiliar word. When reading the word **cloak** for the first time, the brain will divide it into **cl** and **oak** and then use other **o-a-k** words such as **oak** and **soak** to come up with a pronunciation. When a writer is trying to spell **cloak**, however, the brain does a search for rhyming words and may very well come up with **joke** and **smoke** and thus spell **cloak** as **c-l-o-k-e**, Once the writer has spelled **cloak** as **c-l-o-k-e**, if he has ever seen **cloak** before, he might notice it "doesn't look right!" Then his brain goes looking for other rhymes with a different pattern and may indeed find **oak** and **soak**, and he will write that and probably realize that, "Now that looks right!"

The brain has a visual checking system which checks the spelling it generates with what it has seen before. Of course, if a student has never before seen the word **cloak** in print, there would be no way for his brain's visual checking system to work. That is why the ability to use a dictionary (or a spell-checking feature on a computer) to check the probable spelling of a word plays an important role in good spelling.

Students who have mastered Goal Two but need help with Goal Three will be good decoders of one- and two-syllable pattern-following words, but they will often spell words with a possible—but incorrect—pattern. Activities for Goal Three will help students sharpen their visual checking system and learn to use a dictionary to check a possible spelling.

Goal Four

Decoding and Spelling Polysyllabic Words

It is usually painfully obvious when students in upper grades lack this ability. When reading, they stumble over big words and, if you are not standing right there with them, probably just skip the words. When writing, they avoid using any big words they can't spell or, if they can't avoid using the words, they spell the words by "sounding out the letters." Thus, **reaction** is often spelled **r-e-a-c-s-h-u-n.** **Identify** is spelled **i-d-e-n-t-u-f-i. Of all the goals in this book, this is the most common reading and spelling problem for older students. Even many "good" students have a lot of difficulty with polysyllabic words.**

The patterns in words of three or more syllables are not onsets and rimes. Rather they are morphemic units commonly referred to as roots, prefixes, and suffixes. English is the most morphologically complex language. Linguists estimate that for every word you know, you can figure out how to decode, spell, and build meaning for six or seven other words if you recognize and use the morphemic patterns in words (Nagy and Anderson, 1984). **Activities in this section will teach students how to spell a Nifty Thrifty Fifty store of words which contain all the useful morphemes (see list on page 11). They will also help students learn to use these words and the patterns in them to decode, spell, and build meaning for thousands of other words.**

Goal Five

Applying Strategies While Reading and Writing

Finally, we must give students practice in using what they know **about words at the time that knowledge is needed—when they are reading and writing. This transfer step is not automatic and is especially not apt to be automatic for students who have had years to develop "bad habits." For each month, suggestions will be made to help students integrate the strategies they are learning as they are reading and writing.**

The Nifty Thrifty Fifty

Word	Prefix	Suffix
antifreeze	anti	
beautiful		ful (*y-i*)
classify		ify
communities	com	es (*y-i*)
community	com	
composer	com	er
continuous	con	ous
conversation	con	tion
deodorize	de	ize
different		ent
discovery	dis	y
dishonest	dis	
electricity		ity
employee	em	ee
encouragement	en	ment
expensive	ex	ive
forecast	fore	
forgotten		en (double *t*)
governor		or
happiness		ness (*y-i*)
hopeless		less
illegal	il	
impossible	im	
impression	im	sion
independence	in	ence

Word	Prefix	Suffix
international	inter	al
invasion	in	sion
irresponsible	ir	ible
midnight	mid	
misunderstand	mis	
musician		ian
nonliving	non	ing (drop *e*)
overpower	over	
performance	per	ance
prehistoric	pre	ic
prettier		er (*y-i*)
rearrange	re	
replacement	re	ment
richest		est
semifinal	semi	
signature		ture
submarine	sub	
supermarkets	super	s
swimming		ing (double *m*)
transportation	trans	tion
underweight	under	
unfinished	un	ed
unfriendly	un	ly
unpleasant	un	ant (drop *e*)
valuable		able (drop *e*)

Goal One: Learning High–Frequency, Commonly Misspelled Words

If you are working on this goal, it is because many of your students have learned to spell these words in an automatic but wrong way. **Old habits are hard to break and, consequently, only ten of these words will be covered each month.** Each month's list includes words that begin with different letters, some harder words, and some easier words. Here are the ten words for the first month:

because	friends	have	laugh	off
people	said	they	until	want

These words are taken from the list of high-frequency, frequently-misspelled words (see page 7). If all your students would spell some of these words correctly in first-draft writing, you might want to substitute some of the other words on the list, or use high-frequency words not on the list but misspelled by many of your students. **The major activity for learning these words is a Word Wall. Putting the words on the wall is not enough. You have to *do* a Word Wall if you expect your students (many of whom are not strong visual learners) to learn these important words.**

Word Wall

1 **Display the words, arranged by first letter, someplace in the room.** No one ever has enough space or time in a classroom, but clear some space for these important words. Many teachers display the words above or below the alphabet letters over the chalkboard. Other teachers use a bulletin board or hang a banner above a bulletin board and attach the words to it. The words need to be big and bold so that they are easily seen from wherever the students are writing. Using different colors makes them more visible and attractive and is particularly helpful for easily confused words. Many teachers use colored index cards or sticky notes. Regardless of what you write the words on, writing them with a thick, black, permanent marker makes the words much more accessible. (Page 133 shows what your Word Wall should look like at the beginning of the school year, after the August/September high-frequency words have been added. Page 141 shows what your Word Wall should look like at the end of the school year, after all of the high-frequency words have been added.)

In addition to the room display, you might want to give each student a "portable" Word Wall to keep at her desk or to take home. Since the rule is that if a word is on the Word Wall, it must be spelled correctly in all writing in every subject—including homework—a Portable Word Wall is very helpful. You can create this on your own, have the students create their own, or duplicate the "Portable Word Walls" at the back of this book (see pages 133–141). Each month, students get a new list to which the new words (and clues) have been added.

2 **Explain to students that, in English, many of the most common words are not spelled in the logical way.** As you put up each word, have students tell you what is illogical about it. Use questions like these to help them see that these words do not follow the usual patterns: Why is **said** not spelled like **red** and **bed**? Why is **they** not spelled like **pay** and **say**? Where is the double **l** that should be at the end of **until**? and so on.

Talk with students a little about how the brain makes things automatic. Use an example, such as riding a bike or playing an instrument, to which your students can relate. Help them understand that, after doing something a number of times, the brain puts it in the automatic compartment. Explain further that the brain can do many automatic things but only one nonautomatic thing at a time; thus, when a person is writing, these illogical words will go down in the logical way she first spelled them because the nonautomatic thing she is doing is thinking about the ideas she is writing. **Convince students that the problem is not them but the illogical nature of some English spellings.**

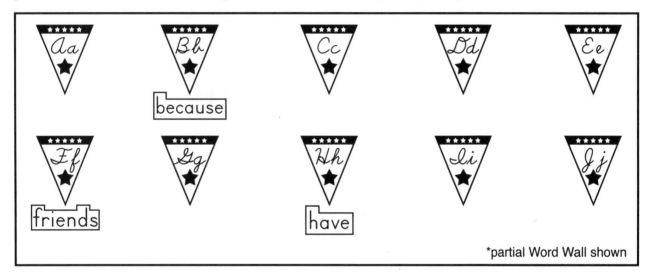

*partial Word Wall shown

3 Explain to students that it isn't really their fault that their brains have learned these words automatically but wrong, but it is their responsibility to fix it. You may want to tell them that the expression, "Practice makes perfect," is wrong. **Perfect practice makes perfect!** Wrong practice makes wrong! Their job now is to have enough practice spelling these words the right way to get the wrong spellings out of the brain's automatic compartment and replace them with the right spellings. The brain, however, did a lot of work to get them in there and is not going to want to give them up!

Tell students that there are two ways you are going to help them get the right practice. First, when you have a few minutes of "down time" in class, you will help them practice the words in a variety of ways. Second, whenever you see a Word Wall word misspelled on anything, you will write WW on that word and return the paper so that the student can fix it and turn it back in. (Acknowledge that you know that they won't like this part but it is for their own good and essential for rooting these words out of the brain's reluctant automatic compartment!)

4 **Tell students that one way to practice words is to say them aloud in a rhythmic chanting fashion.** While this might seem silly to students, it really isn't because **the brain responds to sound and rhythm. That is one of the reasons students can sing along with the words of a familiar song even though they couldn't speak the words without singing, and also why jingles and raps are easy to remember.**

Point to each word on the Word Wall and have students chant it, cheerleader style. Emphasize the "illogical" letters as they chant. Before "cheering" for each word, help students see what is illogical about it:

because	**Because** sounds like it should be spelled **b-e-c-u-z** but is actually logical when you point out the word **cause** and the relationship between **cause** and **because**.
friends	What is that **i** doing there? It may help students if you point out that **friends** "ends" with **ends**.
have	Other **a-v-e** words rhyme with **brave**, **save**, and **wave**. Hundreds of years ago, the word **have** did rhyme with **brave**, **save**, and **wave**. Its pronunciation has changed but it used to be spelled in a logical way! You might want to have students pronounce **have** the old-fashioned way before cheering its spelling.
laugh	There is no reason for **laugh** to be spelled in this funny "laughable" way.
off	This is a totally illogical spelling.
people	This is the only word in which it takes **e-o** to spell the **e** sound.
said	**Said** should rhyme with **paid** and **braid** and it used to. The pronunciation changed but the spelling did not.
they	There is no reason **they** should not be spelled **t-h-a-y** but it isn't!
until	Where is the double **l** that ends all the other rhyming words?
want	Many **w-a** words have a funny pronunciation and follow their own strange **w-a** patterns: **was**, **wad**, **wash**, **war**, **watch**, **warm**, **warp**, etc.

5 Once you have discussed what is strange about each word, given an explanation when possible, and cheered for each word, have students write each word. **Writing the word with careful attention to each letter and the sequence of each letter helps students use another mode to practice the word. (Do not, however, assign students to copy words five times each. They just do this "mechanically" and often do not focus on the letters. Sometimes, they copy them wrong five times, making the automatic wrong spelling even more automatic!) Students enjoy writing the words more and focus better on the word if you make it a riddle or game.** Do this simply by having them number from one to ten and then giving clues to the word you want them to write. Here is an example:

1. Number 1 is the only word with three letters.

2. For number 2, write the four letter word that should be spelled like **say** and **pay**.

3. For number 3, write the four-letter word whose pronunciation used to rhyme with **paid** and **braid**.

4. For number 4, write the four-letter word whose pronunciation used to rhyme with **wave** and **brave**.

5. For number 5, write the four-letter word with the strange **w-a** pronunciation.

6. For number six, write the only word with six letters.

7. For number seven, write the seven-letter word that has the word **cause** in it.

8. The word for number eight has five letters but would have six if it had its logical extra **l**.

9. For number nine, write the totally illogical five-letter word.

10. To end this, write the word that ends with **ends**.

After students have each written the ten words, have them check their own papers by once more chanting the letters aloud, underlining each letter as they say it.

6 Throughout the month, use the chanting and writing activities *(with different clues)* when you have a few minutes of down time to practice the words. Occasionally, ask students what is illogical about the spelling of certain words and help them understand the logic that is there (**said** used to rhyme with **paid** and **braid**) when it exists. Most importantly, when students are writing anything, remind them that the wrong spelling of these words is apt to come out of their brains when their attention is on the meaning of what they are writing. If they notice they are writing one of the words displayed, they should stop and glance at the word to get the correct spelling. If they do misspell these words, you will help their brains root out these words by writing WW on their papers and having them correct the words. They won't like this but, if you are relentless, they will find themselves thinking "WW" as they incorrectly spell one of these words and develop their own self-correction mechanism!

Goal Two: Learning One– and Two–Syllable Words That Follow a Pattern, but Are Used Less Frequently

Many upper-grade students who have not learned basic decoding skills are resistant to any kind of "babyish" instruction. For that reason, and just because it is lots of fun, the **Brand Name Phonics** activities are built around various products and places in the environment. Ideally, you would bring the actual box, can, ad, etc., into the classroom for use in the lessons. Some teachers give students a list of needed products, advertisements, etc., and have students help collect these. Some teachers take photos of products or places and use these to trigger students' interest and awareness that they do indeed see these words in their everyday world. **You may want to use a combination of real containers, advertisements, and photos depending on the words you are using.** After doing each lesson, it is helpful to display the containers, advertisements, photos, etc., on a board somewhere in the room so students will have these words constantly available for reference.

The other activity designed to meet this goal is **Making Words. Making Words is a hands-on manipulative activity in which students learn how adding letters and moving letters around create new words.** Every **Making Words** lesson has a secret word— a word that can be made with all the letters. **Once the words are made, the students sort them into patterns and transfer these patterns to read and spell some new words.**

Brand Name Phonics—Lesson One

For the first lesson, use these three products whose names rhyme: **Snack Pack**®, **Slim Jim**®, and **Shake 'n' Bake**®. By starting with these rhyming products, you can immediately make the point that words with the same spelling pattern usually rhyme. Here is an outline of the first lesson:

1 Begin by displaying the products and letting students talk about them. Do they recognize them, eat them, like them, etc.?

2 Have students identify the product names. Write these names to head three columns on the board or chart. Once the names are all written, help students notice that they rhyme, then underline the spelling patterns **ack**, **im**, and **ake**:

Sn<u>ack</u> P<u>ack</u>®	Sl<u>im</u> J<u>im</u>®	Sh<u>ake</u> 'n' B<u>ake</u>®

Point out to students that many rhyming words have the same spelling pattern. The spelling pattern begins with the first vowel and goes to the end of the syllable.

3 Have each student divide a piece of paper into three columns and head the columns with **Snack Pack®, Slim Jim®,** and **Shake 'n' Bake®,** underlining the spelling pattern in each word. Tell students that you are going to show them some words and that they should write each one under the product name with the same spelling pattern. Show them words which you have written on index cards. Let different students go to the board and write the words there as everyone is writing them on their papers. Do not let the students pronounce the words until they are written on the board. Help the students pronounce the words by making them rhyme. Here are some words to use:

back	dim	cake	take	rack
trim	track	Kim	Tim	snake

4 Explain to students that thinking of rhyming words can also help them spell. This time, do not show the words. Say the words instead, then have students decide with which product each word rhymes and use that pattern to spell it. Here are some words you might pronounce and have students spell:

black	swim	lake	flake	smack
skim	shack	quack	quake	brim

5 End this part of the lesson by helping students verbalize that, **in English, words that rhyme often have the same spelling pattern. Good readers and spellers don't sound out every letter, rather they try to think of a rhyming word and read or spell the unfamiliar word using the pattern in the rhyming word.**

Brand Name Phonics—Lesson Two

For the second part of the lesson, use the same three products and procedure again, but use more complex words:

1 Label the three columns on the board or chart and have students make three columns on their papers with these words, then underline the spelling patterns. Explain to the students that using the rhyme to help read and spell words works with longer words, too.

2 Show students the following words written on index cards and have them write each word under the appropriate product. Once each word is written on the board or chart, have students pronounce the word, making the last syllable rhyme with the product:

victim	shortcake	paperback	horseback	retake
flashback	denim	soundtrack	drawback	feedback

3 Now, say each word below. Have students decide with which product the last syllable rhymes and use that spelling pattern to spell it. Give help with the spelling of the first part if needed.

handshake	outback	blackjack	remake	Muslim
unpack	bookrack	snowflake	hijack	racetrack

4 Again, end the lesson by helping students **notice how helpful it is to think of a rhyming word they know how to spell when trying to read or spell a strange word.**

All the lessons for this goal work in a similar fashion. The steps are as follows:

1. Display and talk about the products.

2. Identify the spelling patterns.

3. Make as many columns as needed on the board and on student papers. Head these with the product names and underline the spelling patterns.

4. Show students one-syllable words written on index cards. Have students write each word under the product with the same pattern, then use the rhyme to pronounce the word.

5. Say one-syllable words and have students decide how to spell them by deciding which product the word rhymes with.

6. Repeat the above procedure with longer words.

7. Help students verbalize how familiar words help them read and spell lots of other words, including longer words.

For some products which have lots of rhyming words, this lesson might take two days. For other products, the lesson might be completed in one session. It is best to spend no more than 15-20 minutes in any one session with a lesson because student attention will waver and because there are lots of other goals to work on.

Brand Name Phonics—Additional Lessons

Here are three other lessons you might do to help students see how lots of words they know will help them decode and spell other words:

Lesson Three
Products: **Spr<u>ite</u>®**, **Diet C<u>oke</u>®**, **gr<u>ape</u>**

One-syllable words to read:
    ape, bite, poke, scrape, tape, quite, stroke, white, choke

One-syllable words to spell:
    kite, spite, broke, smoke, spoke, shape, drape, joke, cape

Longer words to read:
    ignite, provoke, escape, shipshape, unite, invite

Longer words to spell:
    reunite, landscape, polite, impolite, campsite, reshape, revoke

Lesson Four
Products: **Mountain D<u>ew</u>®**, **lemon-l<u>ime</u>**, **r<u>oot</u> beer**

One-syllable words to read:
    chew, dime, shoot, crime, crew, new, snoot, slime, stew, scoot, drew

One-syllable words to spell:
    brew, time, chime, hoot, loot, flew, threw, grime, prime, boot

Longer words to read:
    mildew, nighttime, offshoot, lifetime, renew, anytime

Longer words to spell:
    lunchtime, withdrew, daytime, bedtime, uproot, sometime

Lesson Five

Products: Capri S<u>un</u>®, ginger <u>ale</u>, Ocean Spr<u>ay</u>®

One-syllable words to read:
   stun, stay, stray, sale, scale, tray, gale, whale, play

One-syllable words to spell:
   pale, run, day, shun, spun, shale, male, gray, way, sway

Longer words to read:
   display, portray, impale, overrun, nightingale, begun, female, relay

Longer words to spell:
   rerun, inhale, exhale, repay, replay, outrun, upscale, betray

Making Words—Lesson One

Making Words is a hands-on, manipulative activity in which students learn how adding letters and moving letters around creates new words (Cunningham and Hall, 1994, 1997). To plan a **Making Words** lesson, begin with a "secret" word—a word which can be made from all the given letters. The word for this lesson is **September**. Using the letters in **September**, choose 12-15 words which will provide some easy words, some harder words, and several sets of rhymes. Then, decide on the order in which words will be made, beginning with short words and building to longer words. Write these words on index cards to use in the sorting and transferring parts of the lesson. Write the letters on a strip, vowels first, then consonants, so as not to give away the secret word. Make a copy of the letter strip for each student, or use the reproducible **Making Words Strip** found on page 149.

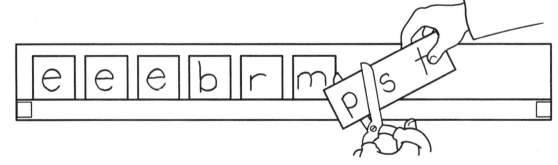

1 To prepare for the lesson, give each student a copy of the strip of letters. Have them cut or tear the letters apart, then write matching capital letters on the backs. Place large letter cards with the same letters along the chalk ledge or in a pocket chart. As students make each word at their desks, choose one student to come and make the word with the big letters.

2 As the lesson begins, the cards with the letters **e**, **e**, **e**, **b**, **r**, **m**, **p**, **s**, and **t** are in the pocket chart. The students have the same letters. Lead students to make words by saying the following:

"Take three letters and make the word **bet**."

"Change one letter to make the word **set**."

"Change **set** into **pet**."

"Now, we are going to make some four letter words. Add one letter to **pet** and you will have **pets**."

"Use the same letters in **pets** to spell **pest**."

"Change where you have these same letters again and spell **step**."

"Now, let's make some five-letter words. Add a letter to **step** to spell **steep**. Steep hills are very hard to climb."

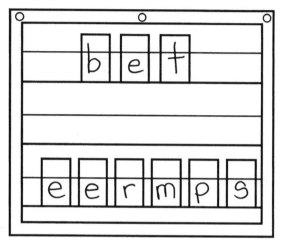

"Make" Step

"Now, spell another five-letter word, **meter**. A meter is a little longer than a yard."

"Let's spell one more five letter word—**reset**."

"Add a letter to **reset** and you will have spelled **preset**."

"Let's spell another six-letter word—**temper**."

"The last six letter word is **beeper**."

"Change **beeper** into a seven-letter word, **steeper**."

"Every making-words lesson has a secret word—a word than can be made with all the letters. Take a minute and see if anyone can figure out the secret word."

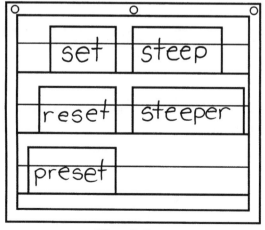

"Sort" Step

If someone figures out **September**, let that student come and make it with the big letter cards. If not, tell the class the secret word and have them all make it.

3 Once all the words are made, lead the students to sort for patterns. For the sorting part of the lesson, put the index cards containing the words in the pocket chart or along the chalk ledge. The first sort is for words with the same root or ending. Pull out the words **set, reset**, and **preset** and talk about how they are all related. Do the same thing for **steep** and **steeper**.

4 Next, help students sort the words into rhymes (see illustration). When the rhyming words are sorted, remind students that rhyming words can help them read and spell unfamiliar words.

5 Write the words **wet** and **sweeper** on cards and have a student place these words in the correct columns. Have students use the rhymes to decode the new words. Finally, help students transfer the pattern to new words. say two more new rhyming words, **creeper** and **vet**, and have the students spell them. Help the students see how the words they made help them spell the new words.

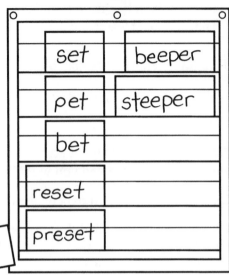

"Transfer" Step

Making Words—Additional Lessons

Here are two other **Making Words** lessons for this month (reproducibles on page 149):

Lesson Two	
Letters on strip:	**Secret Word: birthday** **a i b d h r t y**
Make:	**bid, hid, air, hay, ray, tray, hard, hair, dirt, dirty, hairy, hardy, birth, hybrid, birthday**
Sort for: **y** (ending):	**dirt, dirty; hair, hairy; hard, hardy**
rhyming words:	**hay, ray, tray, birthday** **bid, hid hybrid** **air, hair**
Transfer Words:	**stray, spray, skid, chair**

Lesson Three	
Letters on strip:	**Secret Word: cheeseburger** **e e e e u b c g h r r s**
Make:	**cub, rub, rug, bug, hug, huge, cube, cure, sure, scrub, shrub, shrug, cheese, cheers, secure, cheeseburger**
Sort for: rhyming words:	**cub, rub, scrub, shrub** **bug, hug, rug, shrug** **cure, sure, secure**
Transfer Words:	**smug, stub, pure, plug**

Goal Three: Spelling Words with Two or More Patterns

In English, words that have the same spelling pattern usually rhyme. If you are reading and come to the unknown words **plight** and **trite**, you can easily figure out their pronunciation by recalling other **ight** or **ite** words you can read and spell. **The fact that there are two common spelling patterns with the same pronunciation is not a problem when you are trying to read an unfamiliar-in-print word, but it is a problem when you are trying to spell it.** If you were writing and trying to spell **trite** or **plight**, they could as easily be spelled **t-r-i-g-h-t** and **p-l-i-t-e**. **The only way to know which is the correct spelling is to write it one way and see if it "looks right" or check your probable spelling in a dictionary. What Looks Right** lessons help students learn how to use these two important self-monitoring spelling strategies. **These lessons should only be used once students are quite comfortable with spelling and decoding as outlined in Goal Two. If your students need lots of work with Goal Two, ignore Goal Three until later in the year, then come back and pick up this strand.**

What Looks Right?

For the first lesson, use the **ite/ight** pattern. Below is a description of the steps in an initial **What Looks Right** lesson. Decoding and spelling lessons should not last more than 20 minutes. If students are not familiar with finding words in the dictionary, this will take some extra time. It is well invested time, however, because students need to learn how the dictionary helps with spellings and meanings. Stop the lesson after 20 minutes, collecting papers to continue another day. The first lessons may take three or four sessions but, as students become faster at finding words, the pace will pick up.

1 Write two words which your students can read and spell and which have the **ite/ight** pattern. For this lesson, use **bite** and **fight**.

2 Have students say these words and notice that they rhyme but that they don't have the same spelling pattern. Explain to students that, **in English, using a rhyming word to read another word will work almost all the time, but that spelling is more complicated because some rhymes have two common spellings. Explain that good spellers use a visual checking strategy. After writing a little-used word, they look at it to see if it "looks right."** Ask students if they have ever written a word and realized that it just didn't look right. **Explain that if it doesn't look right, a good speller tries to think of a rhyming word with a different spelling pattern and writes that one to see if it looks right. Finally, if a student needs to be sure of the spelling, he should look it up in a dictionary by looking for it the way he thinks it is spelled.** Explain to students that the activity you are going to do is called **What Looks Right** and will help them learn to check their own spelling the way good spellers do.

3 Create two columns on a chart or overhead and head them with the words **bite** and **fight**. Have the students create these columns on their own papers, writing the words and underlining the spelling patterns **i-t-e** and **i-g-h-t**. Tell students that there are many words which rhyme with **bite** and **fight**. A writer can't tell by just saying the words which spelling patterns they will have. **Explain that you are going to say words and write them using both spelling patterns. Each student should decide which one looks right to her and write only that one. She will then find the word in the dictionary to "prove" it is the correct spelling.**

4 Say a word that rhymes with **bite** and **right** and write it both ways, saying, "If **kite** is spelled like **bite**, it will be **k-i-t-e**; if it is spelled like **right**, it will be **k-i-g-h-t**." Write these two possible spellings in the appropriate columns. Tell the students to decide which one "looks right" to them and to only write the one they think is correct.

5 Once students have committed to a probable spelling by writing the word in one of the columns, have them use the dictionary to see if that spelling can be found. If they cannot find the one they wrote, have them look up the other possible spelling. Erase or cross out the spelling you wrote that is not correct and have students correct their papers if necessary. Continue with some more examples.

6 The next word is **tight**: "If **tight** is spelled like **bite**, it will be **t-i-t-e**; but if it is spelled like **fight**, it will be **t-i-g-h-t**." Write the word both ways and have each student write it the way that looks right. Then have students check the dictionary and correct their spellings if necessary.

7 Use these words next, writing each both ways:

flight	spite	quite	fright	white

Have students commit to a spelling for each word by writing it in only one column, then have them look in the dictionary to find it.

8 Write **site** and **sight** in your columns and, without giving away the fact that both are possible spellings, have students commit and use the dictionary to check. When both spellings are found, have the dictionary definitions read aloud. Help students see how this wonderful tool, the dictionary, can let you know which word to use when two words are pronounced the same but have different spellings and meanings. Next, write **might** and **mite** and reinforce this notion of how the dictionary helps you with sound-alike words.

24

9 In the first part of the lesson, use words students have seen before so they will recognize which "looks right" and know the correct spelling. Later in the lesson, use some words they probably haven't seen. This will help them realize that if they haven't seen a word before they can't tell if it looks right and they really need to check the dictionary. Write these words both ways:

blight	trite	plight

After students find these words in the dictionary, have the definitions read aloud. Help students create sentences to build some meaning for these words.

Explain to students that checking to see if a word looks right, and using a dictionary to check if a spelling is correct, works with longer words, too. Write the following words, whose last syllables rhyme with **bite** and **fight**, both ways. For each word, have students write the spelling they think is correct and use the dictionary to check their hunch.

invite	headlight	ignite	bullfight	excite	dynamite	uptight	eyesight

When you finally finish this lesson—which will take several 20-minute sessions—this is how your board or overhead will look:

bite fight   bite fight
kite ~~kight~~   trite ~~fright~~
~~tite~~ tight   ~~plite~~ plight
~~flite~~ flight   invite ~~invight~~
quite ~~quight~~   ~~headlite~~ headlight
spite ~~spight~~   ignite ~~ignight~~
~~frite~~ fright   ~~bullfite~~ bullfight
white ~~whight~~   excite ~~exeight~~
site sight   dynamite ~~dynamight~~
mite might   ~~uptite~~ uptight
~~blite~~ blight   ~~eyesite~~ eyesight

Have students review these words with you. Help them to summarize what good spellers do—and don't do. **Good spellers don't spell words one letter at a time. They use the spelling patterns they know from other words.** If a written word does not look right, a good speller tries another pattern for that sound. The dictionary helps a student check her probable spelling and lets her know which sound-alike word has the meaning she wants.

Goal Four: Decoding and Spelling Polysyllabic Words

Decoding and spelling polysyllabic words is also based on patterns, but these patterns are more sophisticated. They require that students understand how words change in their spelling, pronunciation, and meaning as suffixes and prefixes are added. The g in **sign** seems quite illogical until you realize that **sign** is related to **signal**, **signature**, and other words. Finding the **compose/composition** and **compete/competition** relationship will help students understand why the second syllables of **composition** and **competition** sound alike but are spelled differently. **To help students learn the system for decoding and spelling big words, students will learn to read, spell, and understand the morphemic composition of 50 words. These 50 words include examples for all the common prefixes and suffixes, as well as common spelling changes.** Because these 50 words will help with so many other words, they are called the **"Nifty Thrifty Fifty"** (see complete list on page 11). The **Nifty Thrifty Fifty** words will be introduced gradually and students will do extensive work with them until their spelling and decoding become automatic. Students will also see and practice lots of other words which can be spelled using the patterns from the words on this list.

The Nifty Thrifty Fifty

This month, eight of the 50 words will be introduced and practiced:

composer	discovery	encouragement	hopeless
impossible	musician	richest	unfriendly

Here are the procedures for working with these words and their important parts:

1 Display the words, arranged by first letter, someplace in the room. No one ever has enough space or time in a classroom, but clear some space for these important words. You may want to use a bulletin board or hang a banner above a bulletin board and attach the words to it. (Note: Display these words separately from the Word Wall words.) The words need to be big and bold so that they are easily seen from wherever the students are writing. Using different colors makes them more visible and attractive. Many teachers use large colored index cards or write the words with different colors of thick, bold permanent markers.

In addition to the room display, you may want to give students a list of these words to keep at their desks or take home. Reproducibles for the monthly **Nifty Thrifty Fifty** words are provided on pages 142–148. Students should get an updated copy of the words each month.

NIFTY THRIFTY FIFTY

composer	discovery	encouragement	hopeless
impossible	musician	richest	unfriendly

2 Explain to students that, in English, many big words are just smaller words with "things," called prefixes and suffixes, added to them. **Good spellers do not memorize the spelling of every new word they meet. Rather, they notice the patterns in words, which include prefixes and suffixes, and spelling changes that occur when these are added.**

3 Tell students that one way to practice words is to say the letters in them aloud in a rhythmic chanting fashion. Explain that while this might seem silly, it really isn't because the brain responds to sound and rhythm. That is one of the reasons students can sing along with the words of a familiar song even though they couldn't speak the words without singing, and also why jingles and raps are easy to remember. Point to each word and have students chant it, cheerleader style, with you. After "cheering" for each word, help students analyze the word, talking about meaning; determining the root, prefix, and suffix; and noting any spelling changes.

composer	A composer is a person who composes something, Many other words, such as **writer**, **reporter**, and **teacher,** are made up of root words with the suffix **er** (meaning a person or thing that does something). When **er** is added to a word that already has an **e**, the original **e** is dropped.
discovery	A discovery is something you discover. The prefix **dis** often changes a word to an opposite form. To cover something can mean to hide it. When you discover it, it is no longer hidden. **Discovery** is the root word **cover** with the added prefix **dis** and suffix **y**. There are no spelling changes.
encouragement	When you encourage someone, you give them encouragement. Many other words, such as **argue/argument** and **replace/replacement**, follow this same pattern. The root word for **encourage** is **courage**. So, **encouragement** is made up of the prefix **en**, the root word **courage** and the suffix **ment**. There are no spelling changes.
hopeless	Students should easily see the root word **hope** and the suffix **less**, Other similar words are **painless** and **homeless**. There are no spelling changes.
impossible	This is the root word **possible** with the prefix **im**. In many words, including **impatient** and **immature** the prefix **im** changes the word to an opposite.

musician	A musician is a person who makes music. A beautician helps make you beautiful and a magician makes magic. **Musician** has the root word **music** with the suffix **ian**, which sometimes indicates the person who does something. There are no spelling changes, but the pronunciation changes. Have students say the words **music** and **musician**, **magic** and **magician** and notice how the pronunciations change.
richest	Students should recognize the root word **rich** with the suffix **est**, meaning "the most."
unfriendly	Students should notice that the prefix **un** often changes a word to its opposite meaning as in **unnecessary** and **unhappy**. The suffix **ly** changes **friend** to **friendly**.

4 Once you have discussed the composition for each word, helped students see other words that work in a similar way, and cheered for each word, have students write each word. Writing the word with careful attention to each letter and the sequence of each letter helps students use another mode to practice the word. (Do not, however, ask students to copy words five times each. They just do this "mechanically" and often do not focus on the letters.) Students enjoy writing the words more and focus better on the word if you make it a riddle or game. You can do this by having them number their papers from one to eight and then giving clues to the word you want them to write. Here are some examples:

1. Number 1 is the opposite of **friendly**.

2. Number 2 is the opposite of **discouragement**.

3. Number 3 is the opposite of **hopeful**.

4. For number 4, write the word that tells what you are if you play the guitar.

5. For number 5, write what you are if play the guitar but you also make up the songs you play.

6. Number 6 is the opposite of **possible**.

7. For number 7, write the word that has **cover** for the root word.

8. Number 8 is what you are if you have the most money of any of your friends.

After students write the words, have them check their papers by once more chanting the letters aloud, underlining each letter as they say it.

5 Throughout the month, use the chanting and writing activities (with different clues) when you have a few minutes of down time to practice the words. As you are cheering and writing the spelling of each word, ask students to identify the root, prefix, and suffix and talk about how these affect the meaning of the root word.

6 Once students can automatically, quickly, and correctly spell all eight words and explain how they are composed, it is time to help them see how these words can help them decode and spell other words. Remind students that good spellers do not memorize the spelling of each word. Rather they use words they know and combine roots, suffixes, and prefixes to figure out how to spell lots of other words. Have the students spell the following words that are contained in their eight words:

compose	pose	discover	cover	encourage	courage
hope	possible	music	rich	friendly	friend

Ask students if they had to make any spelling changes to spell these words. The only spelling change needed here is adding the dropped **e** back to **compose** and **pose**.

7 Next, tell students that you can combine some of the parts of these eight words to spell other words. Have them spell the following words, noting how they are related to the original eight words and noting spelling changes as needed. Help students use each word in a sentence and talk about the meaning relationships when appropriate:

dispose	discourage	discouragement	enrich
enrichment	richly	uncover	hopelessly

Goal Five: Applying Strategies While Reading and Writing

In any classroom, the majority of time available for language arts should be devoted to actual reading and writing. The decoding and spelling strategies described for the first four goals will only be helpful to students if they are reading and writing every day and beginning to employ these strategies as they read and write.

Here are some "reminders" to use as students begin and finish reading and writing activities:

Before Writing:

Say to the students: "As you are writing, concentrate your attention on what you are trying to say—the meaning or message you want to get across. When you finish writing, but before putting your piece away for the day, reread it and look for any Word Wall words that you spelled in the old logical-but-wrong way. Correct these immediately. Look for other words you spelled the best you could but which don't look right to you. Is there another spelling pattern for that rhyme? If you can think of a rhyming word, write it that way and see if that looks right to you."

After Writing:

Ask students to come up with examples of Word Wall words they fixed and/or words that didn't look right and for which they tried a different pattern. Praise their efforts at self-monitoring their spelling and applying what they have been learning during spelling lessons.

Before Reading:

Say to the students: "When we read, everyone comes to words they have heard but have never before seen in print. When you come to an unfamiliar word, stop and say all the letters in that word. Don't try to sound out each letter. Instead, just spell the word to yourself, naming the letters. This allows your brain to search through all its stored words and see if you know a word with the same pattern that will help you figure out the new word. The patterns in some words are the rhymes and in other words are the prefixes, suffixes, and root words. If you come up with a probable pronunciation based on some similar words, try it out and see if it makes sense with what you are reading."

After Reading:

Ask students for examples of words they figured out by saying all the letters and looking in their own "word stores" for words with similar patterns.

Guess the Covered Word

In addition to the before and after reading and writing reminders, an activity called **Guess the Covered Word helps students cross check meaning, word length, and all the beginning letters up to the vowel to figure out words.** To do a **Guess the Covered Word** activity, write some sentences or a paragraph related to something students are studying or a topic of general interest. Select one word per sentence which begins with a consonant letter and cover that word with two torn sticky notes, with the first part covering all the beginning consonant letters up to the vowel. Read each sentence and have students make three or four guesses about the missing word without any letters revealed. Write down these guesses. Remove the sticky note that covers the beginning letter(s). Erase any guesses which are no longer possible and have students make additional guesses for the word that both make sense and have all the right beginning letters. When the students cannot think of any more words that meet both criteria, reveal the rest of the word and see if the correct word was guessed.

To engage the interest of the students, the first **Guess the Covered Word** lessons should use their names and tell things about them that are positive and interesting to kids at this age. Here is an example. Be sure to use *your* students' names and interests.

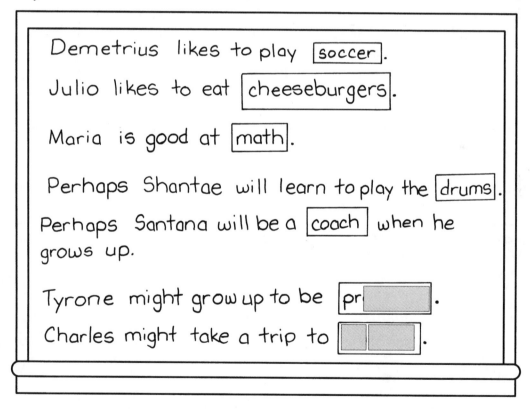

The above shows what a **Guess the Covered Word** lesson might look like after the teacher has led her students to guess the words *soccer, cheeseburgers, math, drums,* and *coach.* The word *president* is ready for the students to guess and uncover after seeing the beginning sound. The word *Chicago* still needs to be guessed and uncovered.

Goal One: Learning High–Frequency, Commonly Misspelled Words

If you have provided some cheering and writing practice, reminded students to check their writing before putting it away for the day, and returned papers with WW's on them, most of your students should have replaced last month's words with correct spellings. **This month's words include more commonly misspelled words, along with the most commonly misspelled homophones and a compound word.**

Word Wall

Here are the new words for this month:

again	could	excited	favorite	into
really	to	too	two	was

As you work with these and future words, follow these procedures:

1 Add the words to your display. Put the word **was** on a different color from last month's word **want**. Use different colors for **to**, **two**, and **too**. In addition, attach a "#2" to the word **two** and a sign saying "TOO late!" to the word **too**.

If desired, give each student a reproduced copy of the Portable Word Wall on page 134 on which the new words (and clues) have been added to previous words.

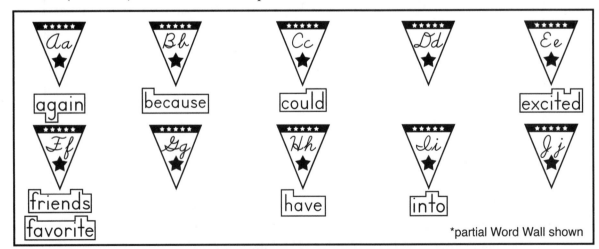

The Word Wall now shows August/September words and new October words.

OCTOBER

② Focus student attention on each word and have students chant it cheerleader style, with you emphasizing the "illogical" letters as they chant it. Before "cheering" for each word, help students see what is illogical about it:

again	There are many words whose first syllables begin with an **a** and are pronounced like **again** (i.e., **about**, **above**, **ago**). The last syllable is spelled like **rain** and **train**. **Again** used to rhyme with **rain** and **train**.
could	There is no explanation for the spelling of **could**. Students may take some consolation in the fact that when they have learned **could**, they can use the same illogical pattern to spell **should** and **would**.
excited	**Excited** is actually the logical spelling but since many people pronounce it as "eg-zited," it just seems illogical!
favorite	The word **favor** is spelled correctly. Many words that end like favorite—**definite**, **opposite**, **granite**—are spelled **i-t-e**.
into	This is a compound word like **inside** and **input**.
really	**Really** combines the word **real** and the suffix **ly**.
to, two, too	Have students notice the clues you attached to two of these words. For the number **two**, point out the related words **twin** and **twice** which also begin with **t-w**. For the "TOO late" **too**, have them pronounce the word emphasizing the **oo**: "You are too—oo—oo late." Tell them that when they find themselves writing this word, they should ask themselves if it is the number 2 or the "too late; too big; too bad" **too**. If it is neither of these, they should use one with no clue—**t-o**. As you have them cheer for these, they should also say the clue: **"t-o—to; t-w-o—number 2; t-o-o—too late"** You might also point out that the "too late" **too** is also the "also" **too**!
was	This is one of those **w-a** words like **want**. **S** at the end of this word sounds like **z**, as in other words such as **is**, **has**, and **does**.

3 Use writing clues to have students write each word. Make sure that your clues distinguish these words from each other and from last month's words. Here are some possibilities:

1. Number 1 is the three-letter word that begins with **w**.

2. For number 2, write the four-letter word that is a compound word.

3. For number 3, write the only eight-letter word on the wall so far.

4. For number 4, write the five-letter word that used to rhyme with **rain** and **train**.

5. For number 5, write the illogical five-letter word that is spelled like **would** and **should**.

6. For number 6, write the seven-letter word that begins with **e-x**.

7. For number 7, write the six-letter word that ends in **l-y**.

8. Write the word that begins with **t** and is a number.

9. Write the word that begins with **t** and is in the phrase "too much."

10. Write the other word that is pronounced just like the words you wrote for 8 and 9.

After they write the ten words, have students check their papers by once more chanting the letters aloud, underlining each letter as they say it.

> **On the day new words are added, practice only those ten. Throughout the month, however, use the chanting and writing activities (with different clues) to practice all 20 words. Do not do more than ten words on any one day but mix them up so that students are continually practicing all the words.** Occasionally, ask students what is illogical about the spelling of certain words and help them understand the logic that is there when it exists. When students are writing anything from now on, they should be held accountable for all 20 words. If they use the wrong **to-too-two**, write WW next to it and let them use the clues to figure out which one was needed.

Goal Two: Learning One– and Two–Syllable Words that Follow a Pattern, but Are Used Less Frequently

Brand Name Phonics

Once again this month, **there are four lessons for helping your students see that words out in the real world can help them read and spell lots of other words. The first two lessons focus on place names and the last two on familiar products.** The steps of each lesson are as follows:

1. Display and talk about the products or places.

2. Identify the spelling patterns.

3. Make as many columns as needed on the board and on student papers. Head these with the product name and underline the spelling pattern.

4. Show the students one-syllable words written on index cards and have them write the words under the product with the same pattern and use the rhyme to pronounce the words.

5. Say one-syllable words and have students decide how to spell them by deciding which product the words rhyme with.

6. Repeat the above procedure with longer words.

7. Help students verbalize how words they know how to spell help them read and spell lots of other words, including longer words.

Lesson One

Places: **Taco Bell**®, **Burger King**®, **Pizza Hut**®

One-syllable words to read:
 fell, shut, bring, yell, sting, string, shell, sell, rut, quell, fling

One-syllable words to spell:
 ring, spring, swell, wing, swing, smell, strut, glut, spell, well

Longer words to read:
 haircut, misspell, firststring, darling, inning, peanut, dumbbell

Longer words to spell:
 retell, shortcut, seashell, something, hamstring, upswing, undercut

Lesson Two

Places: **Wal-Mart**®, **Dollar Store**®, **First Bank**
  (You might substitute local places with **mart**, **store** and **bank** in their names.)

One-syllable words to read:
 thank, tank, tore, prank, part, art, yank, spank, snore, chore, chart

One-syllable words to spell:
 core, smart, rank, crank, start, blank, plank, shrank, shore, score

Longer words to read:
 seashore, outflank, ignore, apart, adore, oxcart, anymore, Mozart, sophomore

Longer words to spell:
 depart, upstart, explore, offshore, outsmart, outrank, restore, drugstore, bookstore

Lesson Three
Products: **Bold**®, **Shout**®, **Cheer**®

One-syllable words to read:
   sold, scout, told, deer, mold, shout, clout, trout, peer, steer

One-syllable words to spell:
   gold, pout, spout, sprout, jeer, sneer, cold, scold, stout, fold

Longer words to read:
   checkout, reindeer, blackout, blindfold, scaffold, knockout, uphold, dropout, engineer

Longer words to spell:
   cookout, without, household, handout, unfold, fallout, withhold, pioneer, volunteer

Lesson Four
Products: **Ivory Snow**®, **all**®, **Tide**®

One-syllable words to read:
   slide, grow, mow, bride, flow, wall, **stride, hide, crow**

One-syllable words to spell:
   hall, wide, glide, show, pride, grow, small, slow, **side, fall**

Longer words to read:
   yellow, collide, borrow, narrow, lumber, decide, divide, **basketball, fluoride, elbow**

Longer words to spell:
   shadow, below, graphic, install, overrule, confide, **below, subside, override, install**

Making Words

Here are the steps for each **Making Words** lesson:

1. Give students the strips which have the letters for the lesson written on them (see **Making Words** reproducibles on page 150.) Have the students cut or tear the letters apart and write matching capital letters on the back. Place large letter cards with the same letters along the chalk ledge or in a pocket chart.

2. Tell students which words to make. Let them know when they just need to add a letter or change the order of letters. Use sentences for words when students might not immediately recognize the meaning.

3. Have one student come and make each word with the big letter cards. Other students should correct their words if they are not spelled correctly. Keep a brisk pace. Do not wait for everyone to make each word before sending someone up to make it with the big letter cards.

4. Give the students a minute to see if they can come up with the secret word. If no one can figure it out, tell them the word and have them make it.

5. Have students sort the words into patterns. Sort first for words with the same root or ending, and then for rhymes.

6. When the rhyming words are sorted, remind the students that rhyming words can help them read and spell words. Write two new rhyming words on cards and have students place these words under the rhyming words and use the rhymes to decode them. Finally, say two new rhyming words and help students see how the previous rhyming words help them spell these words.

Here are three **Making Words** lessons for this month:

Lesson One	**Secret Word: October**
Letters on strip:	e o o b c r t
Make:	cot, cob, rob, rot, toe, oboe, boot, root, core, tore, bore, robe, robot, October
Sort for: rhyming words:	cot, rot, robot cob, rob root, boot core, tore, bore toe, oboe
Transfer Words:	plot, score, throb, shoot

Lesson Two **Secret Word: touchdowns**

Letters on strip: o o u c d h n s t w

Make: to, too, two, tow, cow, how, now, own, out, snow, show, down, town, shout, touch, touchdowns

Sort for: rhyming words: **down, town**

out, shout

cow, how, now

tow, show, snow (Note two pronunciations for **ow**.)

Transfer Words: **plow, clown, grow, sprout**

Lesson Three **Secret Word: footballs**

Letters on strip: a o o b f l l s t

Make: fall, tall, ball, tool, fool, fast, last, soft, loft, aloft, stool, stall, blast, float, ballot, footballs

Sort for: rhyming words: tall, ball, fall, stall
tool, fool, stool
fast, last, blast
soft, loft, aloft

Transfer Words: **cast, drool, school, mall**

Goal Three: Spelling Words with Two or More Patterns

What Looks Right?

Continue using the **What Looks Right** lesson format. Remember that each lesson will take several days until students get quicker at using the dictionary to find words and check spelling and meaning. But remember also that this is a crucial strategy so it is worth the time investment. This month's lesson will be described fully. The months to follow will contain two lessons each in outline form since both you and the students will know the procedures.

Here are the steps for a **What Looks Right** lesson:

1. Write two words on the board which your students can read and spell and which have the **ane/ain** pattern. For this lesson, use **Jane** and **rain**.

2. Have students say these words and notice that even though the words rhyme, they don't have the same spelling pattern. Remind students that, in English, using a rhyming word to read another word will work almost all the time but that spelling is more complicated because some rhymes have two common spellings. Good spellers use a visual checking strategy. After writing a little-used word, they look at it to see if it "looks right." If it doesn't look right, good spellers try to think of another rhyming word with a different spelling pattern and write that one to see if it looks right. Finally, if the writer needs to be sure of the spelling, he can look it up in a dictionary. Remind students that **What Looks Right** will help them learn to check their own spelling the way good spellers do.

3. Create two columns on the board or overhead and head them with the words **Jane** and **rain**. Have the students create these columns on their own papers, writing the words and underlining the spelling patterns **a-n-e** and **a-i-n**. Tell them that there are many words that rhyme with **Jane** and **rain**, and that they can't tell by just saying the words which spelling patterns to use. Remind students that you are going to say words and write them using both spelling patterns. Their job is to decide which one looks right and write only that one. They will then find the word in the dictionary to "prove" it is the correct spelling.

4. Say a word that rhymes with **Jane** and **rain** and write it both ways, saying, "If **train** is spelled like **Jane**, it will be **t-r-a-n-e**; if it is spelled like **rain**, it will be **t-r-a-i-n**." Write these two possible spellings in the appropriate columns. Tell the students to decide which one "looks right" to them and to only write the one they think is correct.

5. Once students have committed to a probable spelling by writing the word in one of the columns, have them use the dictionary to see if that spelling can be found. If they cannot find the one that looked right, have them look up the other possible spelling. Erase or cross out the incorrect spelling you wrote and have students correct their papers if necessary. Continue with some more examples.

6. The next word is **sane**: "If **sane** is spelled like **Jane**, it will be **s-a-n-e**; but if it is spelled like **rain**, it will be **s-a-i-n**." Write the word both ways and have each student write it the way it looks right and then check in the dictionary.

7. Use these words next, writing each both ways:

> **brain**   **lane**   **chain**   **stain**   **gain**   **cane**

Have students commit to a spelling by writing it in only one column, then let them look in the dictionary to find it.

8. Write **plane** and **plain** in your columns and, without giving away the fact that both are possible spellings, have students commit and use the dictionary to check. When both spellings are found, have the dictionary definitions read aloud. Help students see how this wonderful tool, the dictionary, can let you know which word to use when you have two words which are pronounced the same, but which have different spellings and meanings. Next, write **main** and **mane** and reinforce this notion of how the dictionary helps with sound-alike words.

9. In the first part of the lesson, use words students have seen before so they will recognize which ones "looks right" and have the correct spelling. Later in the lesson, use some words they may not have seen, so they realize that they can't tell if an unfamiliar word looks right and they really need to check the dictionary. Write these words both ways:

> **crane**   **Spain**   **sprain**

After students find these words in the dictionary, have them read the definitions aloud. Help students create sentences to build some meaning for these words if necessary.

10. Explain to students that checking to see if a word looks right, and using a dictionary to check a spelling, works with longer words, too. Write the following words whose last syllables rhyme with **Jane** and **rain** both ways. Have students write the one they think is correct and use the dictionary to check their hunch.

> **complain**   **octane**   **hurricane**   **entertain**
> **cellophane**   **contain**   **remain**   **explain**

When you finish this lesson, this is how your chart or overhead will look:

Jane	rain	Jane	rain
~~trane~~	train	~~Spane~~	Spain
sane	~~sain~~	~~sprane~~	sprain
~~brane~~	brain	~~complane~~	complain
lane	~~lain~~	octane	~~octain~~
~~chane~~	chain	hurricane	~~hurricain~~
~~stane~~	stain	~~entertane~~	entertain
~~gane~~	gain	cellophane	~~cellophain~~
cane	~~cain~~	~~contane~~	contain
plane	plain	~~remane~~	remain
mane	main	~~explane~~	explain
crane	~~crain~~		

Have students review these words with you and **help them to summarize what good spellers do—and don't do. Good spellers don't spell words one letter at a time. They use the spelling patterns they know from other words. If a word does not look right, a good speller tries another pattern for that sound. A good speller uses the dictionary to check the probable spelling and find out which sound-alike word has the right meaning.**

Goal Four: Decoding and Spelling Polysyllabic Words

Nifty Thrifty Fifty

Here are this month's new words:

expensive	**governor**	**impression**
independence	**submarine**	**transportation**
	unfinished	

These are the procedures for working with these words and their important parts:

1 Add these words to the display in your room. If you are giving students their own lists, add these or duplicate the list for October (page 143).

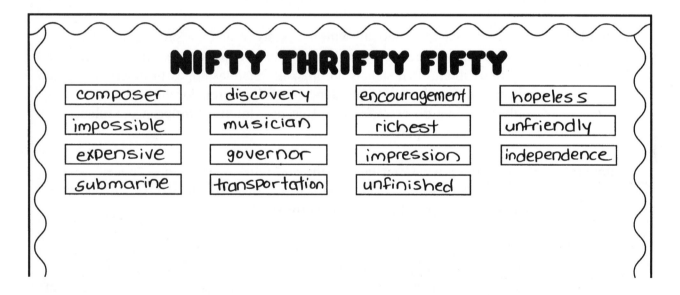

NIFTY THRIFTY FIFTY

composer	discovery	encouragement	hopeless
impossible	musician	richest	unfriendly
expensive	governor	impression	independence
submarine	transportation	unfinished	

2 Remind students that, in English, many big words are just smaller words with prefixes and suffixes added to root words. Explain that sometimes adding these parts requires spelling or pronunciation changes. **Good spellers do not memorize the spelling of every new word they meet. Rather, they notice the patterns in words, including prefixes, suffixes, and spelling changes.**

3 Point to each word and have students chant it, cheerleader style, with you. After "cheering" for each word, help students analyze the word, talking about its meaning; determining the root, prefix, and suffix; and noting any spelling changes.

expensive	This is the word **expense** with the suffix **ive** added and the **e** in **expense** dropped. Another related word which students might not know is **expend**. You might be able to make the **expend/expense/expensive** relationship clear to them by using the commonly-used sports terms **defend/defense/defensive** and **offend/offense/offensive**.
governor	Like **er**, the suffix **or** often signifies the person or thing that does something. The **governor** governs; the **donor** donates; the **actor** acts.
impression	Students will notice the word **impress** with the suffix **ion** added. Because **press** is such a common root, help them to see that **press** actually means "press." When you walk in snow, your footprints press in the snow and make an impression. The impression your attitude makes on people is pressed into their minds. Related words are **depress/depression** in which things are pressed down and **compress/compression** in which things are pressed together.
independence	This is the root word **depend** with the prefix **in** and the suffix **ence**. Help students see that **independence** is the opposite of **dependence**. The prefix **in**, like **im** (**impossible**), often signals an opposite relationship, as in **inactive** and **inconvenient**. The **depend/dependent/dependence** relationship occurs in many words, including **differ/different/difference**, **innocent/innocence**, **violent/violence**, and **patient/patience**.
submarine	This is the root word **marine** with the prefix **sub**, which means "under." A **submarine** goes under water. Other **sub** words in which the **sub** means under include **subfreezing**, **submerge**, and **subway**.
transportation	Students will probably see the word **transport** with the suffix **ation**. Help them to also see the word **port**, which means "bring or carry." Students can relate the meaning of **port** to **export** in which you carry out, **import** in which you bring in and **report**, in which you bring some information back. When you carry things across some place, you **transport** them. Other words in which **trans** means "across or through" include **transmit**, **transfusion**, and **transatlantic**.
unfinished	Students should notice the root word finish with the **ed** ending. The prefix **un** often changes a word to its opposite meaning, as in **unfriendly** and **unhappy**.

4 Once you have discussed the composition for each word, helped students see other words that work in a similar way, and cheered for each word, have students write each word. Writing the word with careful attention to each letter and the sequence of each letter helps students use another mode to practice the word. Students enjoy writing the words more and focus better on the word if you make it a riddle or game. You can do this simply by having them number their papers from one to seven and then giving clues for each word you want them to write. Be sure that your clues distinguish the words from one another and from the eight words on which students focused last month:

1. Number 1 is the opposite of **finished**.

2. Number 2 is the opposite of **dependence**.

3. Number 3 is the highest elected official of a state.

4. For number 4, write the word in which **sub** means "under."

5. For number 5, write the word that contains the root word **port**, meaning "bring or carry."

6. Number 6 is the word that contains the root word **press**.

7. Number 7 is the word that ends in **sive**.

After students write the words, have them check their papers by once more chanting the letters aloud, underlining each letter as they say it.

5 Have students spell and write the following words contained in this month's new words:

govern	impress	press	depend
marine	transport	port	finish
	finished		

6 Next, tell students that you can combine some of the parts of the month's **Nifty Thrifty Fifty** words and spell new words. Have them spell the following words, noting how they are related to the new words, and noting spelling changes as needed. Help students use each word in a sentence and talk about the meaning relationships when appropriate.

express	expressed	expression	export	exported
exportation	governed	impressed	pressed	depended
transported	inexpensive	import	imported	importation

Throughout the month, use the chanting and writing activities (with different clues) when you have a few minutes of down time to practice the words. As you are cheering and writing the spelling of each word, ask students to identify the root, prefix, and suffix and talk about how these affect the meaning of the root word. Include all 15 words (from the first two months' lists) in your activities, but only five to seven words on any one day.

7 Once students can automatically, quickly, and correctly spell all 15 words and explain how they are composed, it is time to help them see how these words can help them decode and spell other words. Remind students that good spellers do not memorize the spelling of each word. Rather they use words they know and combine, roots, suffixes, and prefixes to figure out how to spell lots of other words.

Here are some words students should be able to spell by using parts of all 15 words:

expose	exposed	composed	posed	discovered	covered
encouraged	uncovered	hoped	transpose	transposed	government
		compress	compression		

Goal Five: Applying Strategies While Reading and Writing

Continue to remind your students (and yourself!) that the word strategies they are learning are worthless if they don't begin actually using them to read and write better. Before they write, have them read the Word Wall words quickly and remind them why they are on the wall and being practiced. When students finish any writing assignment, have them reread their work looking for WW words as well as words that don't look right. Remind them to think of other words they know with different spelling patterns to find spellings that "look right."

Before students read, remind them that everyone sees new words in their reading. If they will say all the letters in an unfamiliar word, their brains will search out other words with similar patterns—rhymes, roots, prefixes, and suffixes—which will help them come up with a pronunciation. Remind students to always check their pronunciation to make sure it makes sense and "sounds right." Encourage students to share their spelling and decoding success stories with other students.

Guess the Covered Word

Remember to provide practice with cross checking by occasionally giving students some sentences or a paragraph in which they have to guess some words—first with no letters showing, and then with all the letters up to the vowel. **Students should become good at using meaning, beginning letters, and word length to figure out words.** (See complete directions on page 31.) Here is an example based on an event in which most kids are interested—The World Series:

> After winning the fifth game in a freezing Cleveland, the Florida Marlins were delighted to be heading home to Miami, leading the series 3-2 against the Cleveland Indians. The Marlins only needed to win one more game, and the two remaining games were in their home stadium. Cleveland had to be victorious in game six or the series was over for them. Their shortstop, Omar Vizquel, made a sensational play. Their bull pen shut down the Marlins in the late innings. Manny Ramirez hit two s_____ flies. The Indians had _____ and forced Game Seven.

The above shows what a **Guess the Covered Word** lesson might look like after the teacher has led her students to guess the words *freezing, Florida, remaining, stadium, victorious, sensational,* and *late.* The word *sacrifice* is ready for the students to guess and uncover after seeing the beginning sound. The word *survived* still needs to be guessed and uncovered.

Goal One: Learning High–Frequency, Commonly Misspelled Words

It's a new month and time to root out and replace ten more menacing words! Here are the words for this month:

beautiful	before	enough	first	school
their	there	they're	went	when

This month, students will again learn words for the Word Wall. Then, they will review with a game called **Be a Mind Reader**.

Word Wall

1 Add the words to your display. **When adding words that begin with the same letter, use different colors.** Use different colors for **there**, **their**, and **they're**. Attach a card saying "they are" next to **they're** and underline the **h-e-r-e** in **there**. Provide students with the Portable Word Wall on page 135 on which the new words (and clues) have been added to previous words.

2 Focus student attention on each word and have students chant it, cheerleader style, with you emphasizing the "illogical" letters as they chant. Before "cheering" for each word, help students see what is illogical about it:

beautiful	This is the word **beauty** with the **y** changed to **i** before adding **ful**.
before	This word is actually spelled logically because the **fore** is related to words like **forehead** and **forecast**, not **for**.
enough	Again, there is no explanation for the spelling of the last syllable, but once students can spell it they can also spell **rough** and **tough**!
first	This spelling is quite logical but often misspelled **f-r-i-s-t**!
school	What is that **h** doing there?

there, their, they're　Have students notice the clues you attached to two of these. For the word **there**, explain that you underlined the **h-e-r-e** because this is the word that often means the opposite of **here**.

I was not here. I was there.　　　**Here it is. There it is.**

They're is a contraction for **they are**. Tell students that when they find themselves writing this word, they should ask themselves if it is the opposite of here or if they could write "they are." If it is neither of these, they should use the one with no clue—**t-h-e-i-r**. As you have them cheer for these, they should also say the clue and make a clicking sound and gesture for putting the apostrophe in **they're**:

t-h-e-i-r—their; t-h-e-r-e—there/here; t-h-e-y-'-r-e—they're/they are

went, when　The words are not illogical but are often misspelled **w-i-n-t** and **w-i-n**, especially if pronounced like that.

❸　Use writing clues and have students write each word. Make sure that your clues distinguish these words from each other and from last month's words. Here are some possibilities:

1. Number 1 is the only word we have with nine letters.

2. For number 2, write the word whose last syllable rhymes with and is spelled like **rough** and **tough**.

3. For number 3, write the six-letter word that rhymes with **pool** and **tool**.

4. For number 4, write the four-letter word that begins with **wh**.

5. For number 5, write the four-letter word that rhymes with **tent** and **sent**.

6. For number 6, write the five-letter word that begins with **f**.

7. For number 7, write the six-letter word that begins with **be**.

8. Write the word that begins with **th** and is the opposite of **here**.

9. Write the word that begins with **th** and is a contraction.

10. Write the other word that is pronounced just like the words you wrote for 8 and 9.

After students write the ten words, have them check their papers by once more chanting the letters aloud, underlining each letter as they say it.

4 As the month goes on, use chanting and writing activities to practice all 30 words that have been covered. Do not do more than ten on any one day, but mix them up so that students are continually practicing all the words. Occasionally, ask students what is illogical about the spelling of certain words and help them understand the logic that is there when it exists. When students are writing anything from now on, they should be held accountable for all 30 words. If they use the wrong **to/too/two** or **there/their/they're**, write WW next to it and let them use clues to figure out the correct word.

Be A Mind Reader (A Review of Word Wall Words)

Now that there are 30 words on the wall, there are enough to play a fun game that will give students practice with the words. In **Be A Mind Reader**, think of a word and give students five clues which narrow down the choices to only one possible word. Everyone should get it by the last clue, but did anyone "read your mind" and get it on an earlier clue? Have students number their papers from 1 to 5. Give five clues such as these:

1. *"It's one of our Word Wall words."* (Students hate this but often someone guesses the word and then they love it!) Have them write the word they think you are thinking of next to number 1.

2. *"It has four letters."* (This narrows it down considerably!) If they have a four-letter word for number 1, they would write it again. If not, they need to choose and write a word with four letters.

3. *"It is not a compound word."* (Unfortunately, this only eliminates **into**!)

4. *"It begins with a **w**."* (There are three choices, **went**, **want**, and **what**.)

5. *"It fits in this sentence: I _____ a new bike for my birthday!"*

By now, everyone should have it, but find out who had it earlier and express amazement that they read your mind! Here's another example:

1. It's one of our Word Wall words.

2. It has six or more letters.

3. It is not a contraction.

4. It does not have a **b** in it.

5. It rhymes with **pool** and **cool**.

(school)

Kids love **Be a Mind Reader** and it gives them lots of "painless" practice.

Goal Two: Learning One– and Two–Syllable Words That Follow a Pattern, but Are Used Less Frequently

Brand Name Phonics

This month, use some products in which both words in the name help students read and spell lots of words. It is not necessary to teach all the patterns; once the students start to notice how the words they know will help them, they will begin to use words they haven't yet been taught to use. Older students who have not developed basic decoding and spelling strategies, however, do need lots of practice to overcome their previous failure and ineffective "sound-it-out-letter-by-letter" habits. Remember to follow these steps:

1. Display and talk about the products.

2. Identify the spelling patterns.

3. Make as many columns as needed on the board and on student papers. Head these with the product name and underline the spelling pattern.

4. Show students one-syllable words written on index cards and have them write the words under the product with the same pattern and use the rhyme to pronounce the words.

5. Say one-syllable words and have students decide how to spell the words by deciding which product the words rhyme with.

6. Repeat the above procedure with longer words.

7. Help students verbalize how words they know how to spell help them read and spell lots of other words, including longer words.

Lesson One
Products: <u>i</u>ce <u>cr</u>e<u>am</u>, <u>C</u>ool <u>Wh</u>i<u>p</u>®

One-syllable words to read:
nice, team, steam, stream, slice, school, vice, skip, beam, drool

One-syllable words to spell:
gleam, twice, dream, clip, price, pool, spool, scream, grip, spice

Longer words to read:
mainstream, entice, equip, downstream, sacrifice, gossip, preschool, whirlpool, tulip, partnership

Longer words to spell:
upstream, midstream, turnip, overprice, sunbeam, device, carpool, hardship, friendship, spaceship

Lesson Two
Products: <u>K</u>ool <u>Aid</u>®, <u>popc</u>orn

One-syllable words to read:
horn, cop, raid, worn, drop, maid, prop, fool, shop, born

One-syllable words to spell:
torn, flop, braid, scorn, crop, thorn, tool, stool, paid, chop

Longer words to read:
mermaid, lollipop, unicorn, stillborn, workshop, bridesmaid, prepaid, toadstool

Longer words to spell:
newborn, unpaid, raindrop, gumdrop, acorn, afraid, nonstop, stepstool

Lesson Three
Products: **K<u>it</u> K<u>at</u>®, G<u>old</u>f<u>ish</u>®**

One-syllable words to read:
   spit, split, that, grit, flat, dish, bold, spat, mold, rat

One-syllable words to spell:
   slit, old, hold, wish, swish, quit, chat, hat, hit, brat

Longer words to read:
   admit, profit, misfit, wildcat, credit, democrat, selfish, unselfish, acrobat, blindfold

Longer words to spell:
   permit, visit, combat, outfit, nonfat, catfish, starfish, billfold, doormat

Lesson Four
Products: **Sw<u>eet</u> 'n' L<u>ow</u>®, f<u>at</u> fr<u>ee</u>** (cheese, creamer, or other)

One-syllable words to read:
   bee, street, fee, flee, flow, scat, knee, glow, sheet, splat

One-syllable words to spell:
   tree, three, throw, feet, glee, spree, crow, greet, chat, that

Longer words to read:
   Yankee, discreet, referee, chimpanzee, scarecrow, shallow, employee, parakeet, thermostat

Longer words to spell:
   agree, disagree, degree, oversee, overflow, overthrow, hardhat, bobcat

Making Words

Here are three **Making Words** lessons for this month. Refer to the directions on page 20 and reproducibles on page 151.

Lesson One	**Secret Word: Thanksgiving**
Letters on strip:	**a i i g g h k n n s t v**
Make:	**ink, sink, sank, tank, tang, hang, stink, think, thank, thing, sting, vanish, Thanksgiving**
Sort for: rhyming words:	**ink, sink, stink, think** **thing, sting** **sank, tank, thank** **tang, hang**
Transfer Words:	**spank, shrink, spring, slang**

Lesson Two	**Secret Word: candidates**
Letters on strip:	**a a e i c d d n s t**
Make:	**an, can, tan, Stan, side, tide, tied, died, dance, stance, candies, distance, candidates**
Sort for: rhyming words:	**an, can, tan, Stan** **dance, stance** **side, tide** **tied, died** (Note two spellings for rhyme.)
Transfer Words:	**bride, fried, bran, France**

Lesson Three	**Secret Word: Americans**
Letters on strip:	**a a e i c m n r s**
Make:	**am, ram, Sam, are, ace, race, mace, scram, cream, scream, camera, racism, America, Americans**
Sort for: related words:	**race, racism** **America, Americans**
rhyming words:	**ace, race, mace** **cream, scream** **am, ram, Sam, scram**
Transfer Words:	**cast, drool, school, mall**

Goal Three: Spelling Words with Two or More Patterns

What Looks Right?

This month's lessons use the **eet/eat** and **eel/eal** patterns. Using the words provided on page 56, follow these steps for a lesson:

1. Write two words on the board which your students can read and spell and which have the patterns.

2. Have students say these words and notice that they rhyme but that they don't have the same spelling pattern.

3. Create two columns on a board or overhead and head them with the words, underlining the spelling patterns. Have the students create these columns on their own papers, writing the words and underlining the spelling patterns.

4. As you say each word, write it both ways. Students should write it in the way that looks right to them and then check the word by finding it in the dictionary.

5. Once the correct spelling is verified, erase or cross out the incorrect spelling and have students correct their papers if necessary. Continue with the next word.

6. End the lesson by having students review the words with you. Help them to summarize what good spellers do—and don't do. Good spellers don't spell words one letter at a time. They use the spelling patterns they know from other words. If a word does not look right, a good speller tries another pattern for that sound. The dictionary helps check probable spellings and the writer decides which sound-alike word has the desired meaning.

The first words in each lesson are words for which many students will recognize the correct spelling. When possible, the lesson will contain sound-alike words to provide practice in using the dictionary to determine which word to use when two words are pronounced the same but have different spellings and meanings. Later in the lesson, less common words will be included. This will help students realize that if they haven't seen a word before, they can't tell if it looks right, and they really need to check the dictionary. Each lesson ends with some longer words.

Lesson One	
sw<u>eet</u>	**<u>eat</u>**
~~neet~~	neat
~~seet~~	seat
sheet	~~sheat~~
~~cheet~~	cheat
street	~~streat~~
sleet	~~sleat~~
meet	meat
feet	feat
beet	beat
~~wheet~~	wheat
~~cleet~~	cleat
fleet	~~fleat~~
~~repeet~~	repeat
parakeet	~~parakeat~~
~~defeet~~	defeat
~~heartbeet~~	heartbeat
~~carseet~~	carseat
spreadsheet	~~spreadsheat~~
~~retreet~~	retreat
discreet	~~discreat~~

Lesson Two	
f<u>eel</u>	**m<u>eal</u>**
wheel	~~wheal~~
~~seel~~	seal
~~deel~~	deal
squeel	squeal
heel	heal
steel	steal
peel	peal
reel	real
eel	~~eat~~
~~zeel~~	zeal
~~veel~~	veal
kneel	~~kneal~~
~~reveel~~	reveal
~~conceel~~	conceal
~~appeel~~	appeal
~~repeel~~	repeal
~~misdeel~~	misdeal
~~oatmeel~~	oatmeal
~~unreel~~	unreal
~~ordeel~~	ordeal

Goal Four: Decoding and Spelling Polysyllabic Words

Nifty Thrifty Fifty

Here are this month's new words:

beautiful	classify	community
communities	electricity	happiness
	prettier	

Use these procedures for working with these words and their important parts:

1 Add these words to the display in your room. If you are giving students their own lists, add these or duplicate the list for November (page 144).

2 Remind students that, in English, many big words are just smaller words with prefixes and suffixes added to root words. Sometimes adding these parts requires spelling or pronunciation changes. **Good spellers do not memorize the spelling of every new word they meet. Rather, they notice the patterns in words. These patterns include prefixes, suffixes, and the spelling changes.**

3 Point to each word and have students chant it with you. After cheering for each word, help students analyze the word, talking about meaning and determining the root, prefix, and suffix and noting any spelling changes:

beautiful	This is the word **beauty** with the suffix **ful** added and the **y** changed to an **i**. The suffix **ful** means "full of," as in **painful** and **fearful**. If the word to which **ful** is added ends in **y**, the **y** will change to **i**, as in **merciful** and **plentiful**.
classify	This is the word **class** with the suffix **ify**. Similar words include **glory/glorify**, **note/notify**, and **sign/signify**.
community	The word **community** is the word **unity** with the prefix **com** and the **m** doubled. People who live together in a **community** live together with unity. Other words in which the **com** indicates "with or together" include **combat** (to do battle with), **compose** (to put together), and **compress** (to press together).

---

communities   Words that end in **y** have the **y** changed to **i** and **es** added to make this form of the word, as in **countries**, **counties**, and **cities**.

electricity   This is the word **electric** with the **ity** suffix. Note that the spelling does not change but the pronunciation of the **c** does. (Remember that it was the pronunciation of the **c** than changed in **music/musician**. **C** is a tricky letter. You have to expect it to assume many different identities!) Many words follow the **electric/electricity** pattern, including **acid/acidity, public/publicity,** and **toxic/toxicity.**

happiness   Here is **happy** with the suffix **ness** and the **y** changed to an **i**.

prettier   This is **pretty** with the suffix **er** (meaning "more than") and the **y** changed to an **i**.

4 Once you have discussed the composition for each word, helped students see other words that work in a similar way, and cheered for each word, have students write each word. Writing the word with careful attention to each letter and the sequence of each letter helps students use another mode to practice the word.

1. Number 1 is what makes your lights and TV work.

2. Number 2 is the word that ends in **ful**.

3. Number 3 is the word that means a place where people live together.

4. For number 4, write the plural for number 3.

5. For number 5, write the word that contains the root word **happy**.

6. Number 6 is the word that contains the root word **pretty**.

7. Number 7 is the word that has "class."

After students write the words, have them check their papers by once more chanting the letters aloud, underlining each letter as they say it.

5 Have students spell and write the following words contained in the new words:

| beauty | class | unity | electric | happy | pretty |

Then, tell students that some of the parts of this month's new words can be combined to spell other new words. Have them spell the following words, noting how they are related to the new words and noting spelling changes as needed. Use each word in a sentence and talk about the meaning relationships when appropriate:

beautify	**classiness**	**electrify**	**happier**	**unify**

6 Throughout the month, use the chanting and writing activities (with different clues) when you have a few minutes of down time to practice the words. As you are cheering and writing the spelling of each word, ask students to identify the root, prefix, and suffix and talk about how these affect the meaning of the root word. Include all 22 of the **Nifty Thrifty Fifty** words you have covered, but only five to seven words on any one day.

7 Once students can automatically, quickly, and correctly spell all 22 words and explain how they are composed, provide examples of how these words can help them decode and spell other words. Remind students that good spellers do not memorize the spelling of each word. Rather, they use words they know and combine roots, suffixes, and prefixes to figure out how to spell lots of other words.

Here are some words students should be able to spell by using parts of all 22 words:

unhappy	**unhappier**	**unhappiest**	**unhappily**	**unhappiness**	**prettiest**
hopeful	**beautician**	**electrician**	**classified**	**unclassified**	**classification**
		communication			

Goal Five: Applying Strategies While Reading and Writing

Continue reminding students to use their strategies while reading and writing. Before they do any writing, have them read the **Word Wall** words quickly and remind them why the words are on the wall and why these words are being practiced. When students have finished writing, have them reread their work looking for WW words as well as words that "don't look right." Help them to think of other words they know with different spelling patterns to help them spell words that "look right."

Before students read, remind them that everyone sees new words in their reading. If they will say all the letters in an unfamiliar word, their brains will search out other words with similar patterns—rhymes, roots, prefixes, and suffixes—to help them with pronunciation. Remind them to always check their pronunciation to make sure it makes sense and "sounds right." Help students share their spelling and decoding success stories with other students.

Guess the Covered Word

Refer to the directions for this game on page 31. Remember to provide practice with cross checking by occasionally giving students some sentences or a paragraph in which they have to guess some words, first with no letters showing and then with all the letters up to the vowel. Students should become skilled at using meaning, beginning letters, and word length to figure out words. Here is an example related to computers:

Even though computers have only been widely used for a few **decades**, it is hard to imagine life without them. You can find computers in almost every **school** . Most **businesses** couldn't exist without computers. Computers help people get things done much more **quickly** . When they don't work, however, things come to a **screeching** halt! If you are connected to the Internet, computers can help you research all kinds of **topics** . You can find out how many people live in **Romania**, the size of **China**, or the capital of **Sw**▭ . When you are tired of working, computer games can ▭ hours of entertainment.

The above shows what a **Guess the Covered Word** lesson might look like after the teacher has led her students to guess the words *decades, school, businesses, quickly, screeching, topics, Romania,* and *China*. The word *Switzerland* is ready for the students to guess and uncover after seeing the beginning sound. The word *provide* still needs to be guessed and uncovered.

Goal One: Learning High–Frequency, Commonly Misspelled Words

Word Wall

It is a new month and time to root out and replace ten more words! Here are the words for this month:

7 are	8 can't 10	8 don't	12 won't	16 everybody
15 everyone	13 everything	11 our	9 right	14 write

1 Add the words to your **Word Wall** display. When adding words that begin with the same letter, use different colors. Use different colors for **write** and **right**. Attach a pencil to the word **write** to help students differentiate **write** from **right**. If you are also using the Portable Word Walls, give students the sheet for this month (see page 136) on which the new words (and clues) have been added to previous words.

2 Focus student attention on each word and have students chant it, cheerleader style, with you emphasizing the "illogical" letters as they chant it. Before cheering for each word, help students see what is illogical about it:

are	Other words that end in **a-r-e** rhyme with **care** and **spare**.
can't, don't, won't	These are contractions for **cannot**, **do not**, and **will not**. **Don't forget to have students make a clicking sound and an apostrophe-writing gesture as you chant the contractions.**
everybody, everyone, everything	These are all compound words with **every**.
our	This is spelled logically like **sour** and **flour**; in some parts of the country it is pronounced like **are**. If **our** and **are** are homophones in the dialect of your students, add a clue such as "Our Class" to **our**.
right, write	Students will not need to have the pencil or its function pointed out. Explain that there are other words, such as **wreck** and **wrestling**, which begin with **w-r**.

DECEMBER

3 Use writing clues to have students write each word. Make sure that your clues distinguish these words from each other and from last month's words. Here are some possibilities:

1. Number 1 is the three-letter word that starts with **a**.

2. Number 2 is the three-letter word that starts with **ou**.

3. For number 3, write the contraction that means **cannot**.

4. For number 4, write the contraction that means **do not**.

5. For number 5, write the contraction that means **will not**.

6. For number 6, write the five-letter word you need a pencil to do.

7. For number 7, write the other word that is pronounced just like the word you wrote for 6.

8. Write the eight-letter word that begins with **every**.

9. Write the nine-letter word that begins with **every**.

10. Write the ten-letter word that begins with **every**.

After students write the ten words, have them check their papers by once more chanting the letters aloud, underlining each letter as they say it.

Continue to practice ten words at a time from the complete **Word Wall** using cheering and writing modes. Be diligent in writing WW next to any **Word Wall** word misspelled on anything!

Be a Mind Reader

If you and your students enjoy **Be a Mind Reader,** here are some starters for the month (refer to directions on page 50).

Lesson One

1. It's one of our **Word Wall** words.

2. It has eight or more letters.

3. It has the word **every** in it.

4. It refers to people.

5. It ends with **body**.

(everybody)

© Carson-Dellosa Publ. CD-2405

Lesson Two

1. It's one of our **Word Wall** words.

2. There is at least one other word pronounced just like it.

3. It has five letters.

4. The contraction **they're** is one of the words that is pronounced like it.

5. It is the opposite of **here**.

(there)

Lesson Three

1. It's one of our **Word Wall** words.

2. It does not have a **t** in it.

3. It does not have an **e** in it.

4. It has five letters.

5. It begins with an **l**.

(laugh)

Goal Two: Learning One– and Two–Syllable Words That Follow a Pattern, but Are Used Less Frequently

Brand Name Phonics

Here are some **Brand Name Phonics** lessons for the month. Refer to the directions on page 16.

Lesson One
Products: **candy c<u>ane</u>, jelly b<u>ean</u>, M<u>ounds</u>®, Almond J<u>oy</u>®**

One-syllable words to read:
found, dean, bound, crane, Roy, hound, plane, pound, mean, Jean

One-syllable words to spell:
round, ground, sane, toy, sound, lean, clean, lane, boy, Jane

Longer words to read:
compound, surround, annoy, humane, inhumane, soybean, employ, impound

Longer words to spell:
rebound, decoy, around, insane, unclean, airplane, enjoy, destroy

---

Lesson Two
Products: **Cr<u>est</u>®, Sc<u>ope</u>®, Col<u>gate</u>®, R<u>each</u>®**

One-syllable words to read:
rope, rest, skate, plate, fate, quest, peach, preach, cope

One-syllable words to spell:
hope, rate, crate, slope, vest, slate, beach, bleach, chest

Longer words to read:
telescope, arrest, envelope, suggest, roommate, protest, overreach, eggcrate, tailgate

Longer words to spell:
elope, contest, request, rebate, inmate, invest, inquest, impeach, estate

---

Lesson Three
Products: **Ban**®, **Right Guard**®, **Speed Stick**®

One-syllable words to read:
    brick, bright, plan, night, knight, scan, trick, deed, slick, bleed

One-syllable words to spell:
    quick, span, click, slick, sight, breed, than, seed, fight, fright

Longer words to read:
    Buick®**, exceed, minivan, snowman, succeed, proceed, snowman, toothpick, highlight, yardstick**

Longer words to spell:
    carsick, indeed, began, suntan, misfeed, drumstick, nosebleed, chopstick, delight, moonlight

---

Making Words

Here are three **Making Words** lessons for this month. Refer to directions on page 20 and the reproducibles on page 152.

Lesson One Letters on strip:	**Secret Word: celebrate** **a e e e b c l r t**
Make:	**lab, cab, crab, race, lace, late, rate, crate, trace, brace, relate, rebate, create, bracelet, celebrate**
Sort for: rhyming words:	**lab, cab, crab** **lace, race, brace** **late, rate, crate, relate, rebate, create, celebrate**
Transfer Words:	**space, grab, mate, place**

Lesson Two

Letters on strip:

Secret Word: decorates

a e e o c d r s t

Make:

act, art, dart, cart, care, dare, dear, deer, toad, road, rode, code, erode, actor, react, secret, decorates

Sort for: related words:

act, actor, react

rhyming words:

art, dart, cart
care, dare
code, rode
road, toad (Note two spellings for rhyme.)

Transfer Words:

smart, glare, chart, square

Lesson Three

Letters on strip:

Secret Word: relaxation

a a e i o l n r t x

Make:

ax, tax, taxi, rain, rail, next, exit, extra, train, trail, relax, ration, toenail, relation, relaxation

Sort for: related words:

relax, relaxation

tion words:

ration, relation relaxation

rhyming words:

ax, tax, relax
rain, train
rail, trail, toenail

Transfer Words:

strain, sax, frail, sprain

Looks **Right**

Looks **Right**

Goal Three: Spelling Words with Two or More Patterns

What Looks Right?

This month's lessons use the **oat/ote** and **aid/ade** patterns. The word lists are provided on page 68. Here are the steps for a lesson:

1. Write two words on the chart which students can read and spell and which have the patterns.

2. Have students say these words and notice that they rhyme but don't have the same spelling patterns.

3. Create two columns on a chart or overhead and head them with the words, underlining the spelling patterns. Have the students create these columns on their own papers, writing the words and underlining the spelling patterns.

4. As you say each word, write it both ways. Students should write it in the way that looks right to them and then check the word by finding it in the dictionary.

5. Once the correct spelling is verified, erase or cross out the spelling you wrote that is not correct and have students correct their spellings if necessary. Continue with the next word.

6. End the lesson by having students review the words with you. Help them to summarize what good spellers do—and don't do. Good spellers don't spell words one letter at a time. They use the spelling patterns they know from other words. If a word does not look right, a good speller tries another pattern for that sound. The dictionary helps check probable spellings and the writer decides which sound-alike word has the desired meaning.

The first words in each lesson are words for which many students will recognize the correct spelling. When possible, the lesson will contain sound-alike words. These will provide practice in using the dictionary to decide which word to use when two words are pronounced the same but have different spellings and meanings. Later in the lesson, less common words will be included. This will help students realize that if they haven't seen a word before, they can't tell if it looks right and they really need to check the dictionary. Each lesson ends with some longer words.

Looks **Right**

Looks **Right**

Lesson One

c<u>oa</u>t	n<u>ote</u>
boat	~~bote~~
~~voat~~	vote
float	~~flote~~
goat	~~gote~~
~~quoat~~	quote
~~wroat~~	wrote
throat	~~throte~~
oat	~~ote~~
bloat	~~blote~~
gloat	~~glote~~
~~toat~~	tote
~~doat~~	dote
~~devoat~~	devote
~~promoat~~	promote
~~remoat~~	remote
rowboat	~~rowbote~~
scapegoat	~~scapegote~~
~~outvoat~~	outvote
~~misquoat~~	misquote
raincoat	~~raincote~~

Lesson Two

<u>ai</u>d	gr<u>ade</u>
paid	~~pade~~
~~traid~~	trade
~~shaid~~	shade
braid	~~brade~~
~~faid~~	fade
raid	~~rade~~
maid	made
~~blaid~~	blade
~~jaid~~	jade
~~spaid~~	spade
afraid	~~afrade~~
~~barricaid~~	barricade
~~lemonaid~~	lemonade
~~paraid~~	parade
~~grenaid~~	grenade
~~invaid~~	invade
~~arcaid~~	arcade
mermaid	~~mermade~~
~~serenaid~~	serenade

Goal Four: Decoding and Spelling Polysyllabic Words

Nifty Thrifty Fifty

Here are this month's new words:

continuous	**conversation**	**forgotten**
nonliving	**swimming**	**unpleasant**
	valuable	

These are the procedures for the activity:

1 Add these words to the display in your room. If you are giving students their own list, add these or duplicate the list for December (page 145).

2 Remind students that, in English, many big words are just smaller words with prefixes and suffixes added to root words. Sometimes adding these parts requires spelling or pronunciation changes. Good spellers do not memorize the spelling of every new word they meet. Rather, they notice the patterns in words. These patterns include prefixes, suffixes, and spelling changes.

3 Point to each word and have students chant it, cheerleader style, with you. After cheering for each word, help students analyze the word, talking about meaning and determining the root, prefix, and suffix and noting any spelling changes.

continuous	This is the word **continue** with the suffix **ous** added and the **e** dropped. Other common words containing a root word and **ous** include **nervous**, **dangerous**, and **humorous**.
conversation	Here is the word **converse** with the suffix **ation** and the **e** dropped. Similar words include **reservation**, **invitation**, and **conservation**.
forgotten	This is the word **forgot** with the suffix **en** and the **t** doubled. Similar words include **rotten**, **hidden**, and **forbidden**.

nonliving	**Nonliving** is the word **live** with the prefix **non**, the ending **ing**, and the **e** dropped. Other words in which **non** signals an opposite relationship include **nonfattening**, **nonsense, nonprofit**, and **nonfiction**.
swimming	This is the word **swim** with the ending **ing** and the **m** doubled. Similar words include **running, jogging, rapping,** and **drumming**.
unpleasant	This is the word **please** with the prefix **un**, the suffix **ant**, and the **e** dropped. Help students notice the change in pronunciation from **please** to **pleasant**. **Un** is the most common prefix signalling an opposite relationship.
valuable	**Valuable** is the word **value** with the suffix **able** and the **e** dropped. Have students identify the root words and spelling changes in similar words, such as **reliable, likable,** and **flammable**.

4 Once you have discussed the composition of each word, helped students see other words that work in a similar way, and cheered for each word, have students write each word using clues like these:

1. Number 1 is the opposite of **pleasant**.

2. Number 2 is the opposite of **living**.

3. Number 3 is the word that ends in **ous**.

4. For number 4, write the word whose root word is **converse**.

5. For number 5, write the word that contains the root word **forgot**.

6. Number 6 is the word that contains the root word **swim**.

7. Number 7 is the word that ends in **able**.

After students write the words, have them check their papers by once more chanting the letters aloud, underlining each letter as they say it.

5 Have students spell and write the following words contained in the new words:

continue	converse	forgot	living	live
swim	pleasant	please	value	

6 Next, have them spell the following words, noting how these are related to their new words and noting spelling changes as needed. Use each word in a sentence and talk about the meaning relationships when appropriate:

livable	unlivable	continuing	conversing	valuing

7 Throughout the month, use the chanting and writing activities when you have a few minutes of down time to practice the words. As you are cheering and writing the spelling of each word, ask students to identify the root, prefix, and suffix. Talk about how these affect the meaning of the root word. Include all 29 words in your activities but only five to seven words on any one day. Because these words are intended to be models for decoding and spelling thousands of other big words, it is critical that students "overlearn" the spelling and morphemic composition of these words so that they can automatically access these words to help them with other words. Your students should be able to spell and analyze these words quickly, correctly, and without hesitation. Provide as much practice as needed to achieve this goal.

8 Once students can automatically, quickly, and correctly spell all 29 words and explain to you how they are composed, they should be able to spell these words by using parts of all 29 words:

impressionable	unimpressionable	classifiable
unclassifiable	governable	ungovernable
transportable	portable	classification
electrification	communication	depressant
important	classifying	hoping
encouraging	discovering	composing
finishing	transporting	depending

Goal Five: Applying Strategies While Reading and Writing

By now you should be seeing some definite improvement in students' contextual spelling and decoding skills. Continue to urge them to read their writing before putting it up each day and to look for WW words and other words that "don't look right." You might want them to find one word each day which they don't think they have spelled correctly and use their dictionary skills to find the appropriate spelling. When students are reading, encourage them to say each letter of an unfamiliar word, search their mental word stores for similar words, and check pronunciation with context. Ask them to write down one word from the day's reading selection which they decoded using these strategies and let them "brag about" how they got it!

Guess the Covered Word

Holidays and vacations will peak the interest of many students. Perhaps you could use a paragraph about some "fantasy" vacations you and your students would like to take (refer to the directions for **Guess the Covered Word** on page 31):

> Imagine that we could go anywhere and do anything we wanted over the holiday break! Thomas might go to **Disney World®.** Rasheed might enjoy **snorkeling** in the Bahamas. Corinda might enjoy watching the **porpoises** at Sea World®. David might go to Hawaii and surf the **crashing** waves. Santana might hike into the mountains and camp by **streams.** Michelle might like to relax and read **m⬛⬛⬛⬛⬛** . Your teacher might like to stay up late watching old movies and eating ⬛⬛⬛⬛⬛ .

The above shows what a **Guess the Covered Word** lesson might look like after the teacher has led her students to guess the words *Disney World®*, *snorkeling*, *porpoises*, *crashing*, and *streams*. The word *mysteries* is ready for the students to guess and uncover after seeing the beginning sound. The word *chocolates* still needs to be guessed and uncovered.

Goal One: Learning High–Frequency, Commonly Misspelled Words

Word Wall

It is a new month and time to root out and replace ten more "pesky" words! These are the words for this month:

about	except	knew	new	know
no	myself	then	usually	what

1 Add the words to your display. When adding words that begin with the same letter, use different colors. Use different colors for **knew**, **new**, **know**, and **no**. Attach cards saying "old" and "yes" to **new** and **no**. If you are also using the Portable Word Walls, give students a new sheet to which the new words (and clues) have been added to the previous words (reproducible, page 137).

2 Focus student attention on each word and have students chant it, cheerleader style, emphasizing the "illogical" letters as they chant. Before cheering for each word, help students see what is illogical about it:

about	This is another word, like **again**, in which the beginning syllable is spelled with an **a**.
except	This word starts with **ex** like **excited** and then rhymes with and is spelled like **kept** and **slept**.
knew, new, know, no	Here are two more pairs of words pronounced the same but with different meanings. A few other words in English, such as **knock**, **knee**, **knit**, and **knuckle**, begin with **kn**.
myself	Students may recognize this compound word with **my** and **self**. Other compounds with **self** include **yourself** and **himself**.
then	**Then** is spelled logically but often misspelled as **t-h-i-n** or **t-h-a-n**, particularly if pronounced like those words.

| usually | This is **usual** with **ly** added at end like **really**. |
| what | Other words spelled like this rhyme with **at**, **cat**, and **that**. |

3 Use writing clues to have students write each word. Make sure that your clues distinguish these words from each other and from last month's words. Here are some possibilities:

1. Number 1 is a five-letter word that starts with **a** and ends with **t**.

2. Number 2 is the four-letter word that starts with **wh** and ends with **t**.

3. For number 3, write the opposite of **yes**.

4. For number 4, write the other word that is pronounced just like the word you wrote for number 3.

5. For number 5, write the opposite of **old**.

6. For number 6, write the other word that is pronounced just like the word you wrote for number 5.

7. For number 7, write the seven-letter word that ends in **ly**.

8. Write the compound word that ends in **self**.

9. Write the six-letter word that begins with **ex**.

10. Write the **th** word that rhymes with **ten** and **men**.

After students write the ten words, have them check their papers by once more chanting the letters aloud, underlining each letter as they say it.

Continue to practice words by cheering and writing when you have time. Hold students accountable in their writing for all **Word Wall** words. If you have been resolute, you should be seeing consistent improvement in the spelling of these high-frequency words in their writing.

Be a Mind Reader

Here are a few **Be a Mind Reader** possibilities for this month. (Refer to directions for **Be a Mind Reader** on page 50):

Lesson One

1. It's one of our **Word Wall** words.

2. It begins with **th**.

3. It is not a contraction.

4. It has four letters.

5. It rhymes with **pay** and **say** but is not spelled like they are.

(they)

Lesson Two

1. It's one of our **Word Wall** words.

2. It is a contraction.

3. It has four letters.

4. It is not **won't**.

5. It is the opposite of **can**.

(can't)

Lesson Three

1. It's one of our **Word Wall** words.

2. It begins with an **e**.

3. It is not a compound word.

4. It begins with **ex**.

5. It fits in this sentence: I like every vegetable _____ spinach.

(except)

Goal Two: Learning One– and Two–Syllable Words That Follow a Pattern, but Are Used Less Frequently

Brand Name Phonics

Refer to the directions on page 16. Here are some lessons for this month:

Lesson One
Product: **White Rain® hair spray**

One-syllable words to read:
> **spite, brain, drain, write, train, tray, stray, pair, fair, flair**

One-syllable words to spell:
> **air, kite, gain, grain, stay, stair, stain, strain, quite, chair**

Longer words to read:
> **excite, dynamite, explain, unite, decay, entertain, display, despair, repair, restrain**

Longer words to spell:
> **relay, replay, rewrite, reunite, remain, contain, complain, invite, ignite, unfair**

Lesson Two
Products: **Ginger Snaps®, Wheat Thins®, Fudge Stripes®**

One-syllable words to read:
> **grin, gripe, cheat, rap, wrap, skin, scrap, ripe, neat, pleat**

One-syllable words to spell:
> **thin, pipe, chap, chin, treat, trap, strap, wipe, swipe, beat**

Longer words to read:
> **dolphin, sideswipe, pumpkin, handicap, unwrap, bearskin, wiretap, hoofbeat, offbeat**

Longer words to spell:
> **begin, napkin, kidnap, within, hubcap, bagpipe, overeat, overheat, pinstripe**

Lesson Three
Products: **D<u>o</u>g Ch<u>ow</u>®**, **P<u>ine</u> Sol®**, **lemon<u>a</u>de**

One-syllable words to read:
    jog, dine, plow, vow, frog, mine, hog, whine, shade, grade

One-syllable words to spell:
    log, clog, shine, shrine, brow, trade, line, blade, cow, wow

Longer words to read:
    watchdog, somehow, catalog, confine, persuade, bulldog, streamline, eyebrow, blockade, allow

Longer words to spell:
    underdog, airline, eggnog, combine, upgrade, recline, invade, anyhow, endow

Making Words

Here are three lessons for January (refer to directions on page 20 and reproducibles on page 153):

Lesson One	**Secret Word: blizzards**
Letters on strip:	**a i b d l r s z z**
Make:	**lid, rid, bid, bad, sad, lad, lab, slab, drab, Brad, slid, arid, lizard, blizzards**
Sort for: rhyming words:	**lid, rid, bid, slid, arid** **bad, sad, lad** **lab, slab, drab**
Transfer Words:	**skid, grab, crab, mad**

Lesson Two Secret Word: snowstorms

Letters on strip: o o m n r s s s t w

Make: mow, snow, stow, soon, moon, moss, toss, torn, worn, worm, worst, storm, swoon, snowstorms

Sort for: rhyming words:
mow, snow, stow
soon, moon, swoon
moss, toss
torn, worn

Transfer Words: born, cross, spoon, grow

Lesson Three Secret Word: hibernation

Letters on strip: a e i i o b h n n r t

Make: hit, hire, tire, neat, beat, hero, orbit, other, nation, ration, intern, inherit, inhabit, another, hibernation

Sort for: related words: other, another

tion words: ration, nation, hibernation

rhyming words:
hire, tire
neat, beat
hit, orbit, inherit, inhabit

Transfer Words: spit, wheat, wire, treat

Goal Three: Spelling Words With Two or More Patterns

What Looks Right?

This month's lessons use the **ace/ase** and **ear/eer** patterns. The word lists are provided on page 80. The steps for a lesson are as follows:

1. Write two words on the board which your students can read and spell and which have the patterns.

2. Have students say these words and notice that the words rhyme but that they don't have the same spelling pattern.

3. Create two columns on a chart or overhead and head them with the words, underlining the spelling patterns. Have the students create these columns on their own papers, writing the words and underlining the spelling patterns.

4. As you say each word, write it both ways. Students should write it in the way that looks right to them and then check the word by finding it in the dictionary.

5. Once the correct spelling is verified, erase or cross out the spelling you wrote that is not correct and have students correct their spelling if necessary. Continue with the next word.

6. End the lesson by having students review the words with you. Help them to summarize what good spellers do—and don't do. Good spellers don't spell words one letter at a time. They use the spelling patterns they know from other words. If a word does not look right, a good speller tries another pattern for that sound. The dictionary helps writers check probable spellings and determine which sound-alike word has the desired meaning.

The first words in each lesson are words for which many students will recognize the correct spelling. When possible, the lesson will contain sound-alike words to provide practice in using the dictionary to distinguish between two words which are pronounced the same but have different spellings and meanings. Later in the lesson, less common words will be included. Students should realize that if they haven't seen a word before, they can't tell if it looks right and they really need to check the dictionary. Each lesson ends with some longer words.

Lesson One	
r<u>ace</u>	**<u>chase</u>**
place	~~plase~~
ace	~~ase~~
~~cace~~	case
space	~~spase~~
trace	~~trase~~
~~bace~~	base
face	~~fase~~
brace	~~brase~~
pace	~~pase~~
~~vace~~	vase
grace	~~grase~~
lace	~~lase~~
replace	~~replase~~
misplace	~~misplase~~
embrace	~~embrase~~
~~bookcace~~	bookcase
fireplace	~~fireplase~~
disgrace	~~disgrase~~
shoelace	~~shoelase~~
~~suitcace~~	suitcase

Lesson Two	
<u>ear</u>	**<u>cheer</u>**
fear	~~feer~~
near	~~neer~~
~~stear~~	steer
spear	~~speer~~
clear	~~cleer~~
year	~~yeer~~
rear	~~reer~~
hear	~~heer~~
dear	deer
~~vear~~	veer
~~snear~~	sneer
gear	~~geer~~
~~carear~~	career
appear	~~appeer~~
~~reindear~~	reindeer
~~pionear~~	pioneer
~~voluntear~~	volunteer
~~enginear~~	engineer
overhear	~~overheer~~
disappear	~~disappeer~~

Goal Four: Decoding and Spelling Polysyllabic Words

Nifty Thrifty Fifty

Here are this month's new words:

dishonest	illegal	irresponsible
misunderstood	performance	rearrange
	replacement	

These are the procedures for working with these words and their important parts:

1 Add these words to the display in your room. If you are giving students their own list, add these or duplicate the list for January (page 146).

2 Remind students that, in English, many big words are just smaller words with prefixes and suffixes added to root words. Sometimes adding these parts requires spelling or pronunciation changes. Good spellers do not memorize the spelling of every new word they meet. Rather, they notice the patterns in words. These patterns include prefixes, suffixes, and spelling changes.

3 Point to each word and have students chant it, cheerleader style, with you. After cheering for each word, help students analyze the word, talking about meaning and determining the root, prefix, and suffix, and noting any spelling changes.

dishonest	This is the word **honest** with the prefix **dis** signalling an opposite relationship.
illegal	This is the word **legal** with the prefix **il** signalling an opposite relationship. Similar words include **illiterate** and **illegitimate**.
irresponsible	Here is the word **response** with the prefix **ir** signalling an opposite relationship and the suffix **ible** with the **e** dropped. If you are **irresponsible**, you are not able to make the correct response or to take responsibility. Similar words include **irregular** and **irrational**. Students should know that the **im** in **impossible**, **in** in **independence**, **il** in **illegal**, and **ir** in **irresponsible** all change these words to opposites.

misunderstood — Here, the word **understood** (past of **understand**) has the prefix **mis**, signalling an opposite relationship. The prefix **mis** often signals an opposite relationship and also has a "bad" or "wrong" meaning as in **mistake**, **miscarriage**, and **misdemeanor**.

performance — This is the word **perform** with the suffix **ance**. The actual root word is **form**, meaning "shape or form." When you **reform** something, you make it again (and supposedly better). Something that is **deformed** has had its shape or form damaged.

rearrange — **Rearrange** is simply **arrange** with the prefix **re** meaning "again."

replacement — **Place** has the addition of the suffix **ment** and the prefix **re**. In this case, **re** means "back." When you **replace** something, you put something back where something was before.

4 Once you have discussed the composition for each word, helped students see other words that work in a similar way, and cheered for each word, have students write each word. Use clues like these:

1. Number 1 is the opposite of **responsible**.
2. Number 2 is the opposite of **legal**.
3. Number 3 is the opposite of **honest**.
4. For number 4, write the word in which **mis** means "bad" or "wrong."
5. For number 5, write the word that contains the root word **form**.
6. Number 6 is the word that contains the root word **place**.
7. Number 7 is the nine-letter word in which **re** means "again."

After students write the words, have them check their papers by once more chanting the letters aloud, underlining each letter as they say it.

5 Have students spell and write the following words contained in the new words for the month:

honest	legal	responsible	response	understood
perform	form	arrange	replace	place
		stood		

6 Next, have students spell the following words, noting how they are related to the new words and noting spelling changes as needed. Use each word in a sentence and talk about the meaning relationships when appropriate:

displace	displacement	reform	rearrangement	misplace

7 Throughout the month, use the chanting and writing activities to practice the words. As you are cheering and writing the spelling of each word, ask students to identify the root, prefix, and suffix and talk about how these affect the meaning of the root word. Include all the words you have covered in your activities, but only five to seven words on any one day. Remember to work for quick, fluent, correct spelling and analysis of all 36 words so that your students have instant access to these words to use in decoding and spelling other words. Here are some words they should now be able to spell:

conform	conformity	inform	informer	informant
information	misinform	uninformed	formation	formal
transform	transformation	performer	responsibility	responsive
responsiveness	honesty	dishonesty	honestly	legally
illegally	responsibly	irresponsibly	arranging	rearranging
placing	replacing	misplacing	report	reporter
refinish	relive	repose	reclassify	revalue
recover	rediscover	electrical	displease	discontinue
		irreplaceable*		

*The **e** is not dropped because pronunciation of **c** would change if it were.

Goal Five: Applying Strategies While Reading and Writing

Continue to encourage transfer of strategies to real reading and writing. If possible, have students look back at writing done earlier in the year and see for themselves how their spelling is improving.

Guess the Covered Word

Remember to provide practice with cross checking by occasionally giving students a paragraph in which they have to guess some words, first with no letters showing and then with all the letters up to the vowel (see complete directions, page 31). Students should become skilled at using meaning, beginning letters, and word length to figure out words. Here is an example related to the Martin Luther King, Jr. holiday:

> Martin Luther King, Jr., was one of the nation's leaders in the **struggle** for civil rights. He was born in Atlanta, Georgia, on January **fifteenth** , 1929. His father and grandfather were both **preachers** and another grandfather was a **sharecropper** . King **promoted** nonviolence and led the Montgomery, Alabama bus boycott. King was often the **target** of violence. He was **stabbed** in New York City and pelted with **stones** in Chicago. In 1964, he was the **recipient** of the Nobel Peace Prize for **leading** the movement for equality. MLK was shot and **k** on April 4, 1968. James Earl Ray guilty to murder, but some people believe Ray was not the assassin.

The above shows what a **Guess the Covered Word** lesson might look like after the teacher has led her students to guess the words *struggle, fifteenth, preachers, sharecropper, promoted, target, stabbed, stones, recipient,* and *leading.* The word *killed* is ready for the students to guess and uncover after seeing the beginning sound. The words *pleaded* and *sole* still need to be guessed and uncovered.

FEBRUARY

Goal One: Learning High–Frequency, Commonly Misspelled Words

Here are the new words for February:

by	buy	didn't	doesn't	especially
something	sometimes	who	one	won

Word Wall

1 Add the words to your display. **If you are using different colors, you may be running out of colors for those troublesome, omnipresent "w" words. Repeat colors if needed, but be sure to put homophones on different colors.** Attach clues with the number **1** next to **one** and the word "sell" next to **buy**. If you are also using the Portable Word Walls, give students a new sheet to which the new words (and clues) have been added (reproducible on page 138).

2 Focus student attention on each word and have students chant it, cheerleader style, with you. Before cheering for each word, point out helpful clues and illogicalities!

by, buy; one, won	By now, students should not need any explanation of how the clues you are attaching help them know which word to use.
didn't, doesn't	Students should figure out that these are contractions for **did not** and **does not**. Remember to click and gesture for the apostrophe when cheering.
especially	Point out the word **special** and the ending **ly** as in **really** and **usually**.
something, sometimes	These are compound words with **some**. Other compounds include **someone** and **somebody**,
who	This is a totally illogical spelling for this word.

3 Use writing clues to have students write each word:

1. Number 1 is a three-letter number word.

2. Number 2 is the other three-letter word pronounced just like number 1.

3. For number 3, write the opposite of **sell**.

4. For number 4, write the other word that is pronounced just like the word you wrote for 3.

5. For number 5, write the illogically-spelled, three-letter word that starts with **wh**.

6. This word starts with **some** and rhymes with **ring**.

7. Write the other compound word that starts with **some**.

8. This word has something very **special** in it.

9. Write the five-letter contraction that starts with **d**.

10. Write the six-letter contraction that starts with **d**.

After students write the ten words, have them check their papers by once more chanting the letters aloud, underlining each letter as they say it.

The Wheel

In addition to **Be a Mind Reader** (see page 50), students will enjoy playing **The Wheel** with the **Word Wall** words. To play **The Wheel**, draw blanks on the board to represent the letters in a **Word Wall** word. Have students draw the same number of blanks on their own papers. Go around the class, letting students ask for letters. If the letter is there, write it in the appropriate blank and let the student ask again. Students can continue asking until they ask for a letter that is not in the word. Then go on to the next student. The winner is the first person to spell the whole word correctly and the winner becomes the "teacher" for the next lesson. Here is an example:

1. The teacher draws five blanks on the board and says, "Our first word has five letters. Billy, guess a letter."

2. Billy asks for a **t**. There is no **t** so the teacher moves on to Carol, who asks for an **s**. There is no **s** either. Nor is there an **e**, for which Kevin asks. Sarah asks for and gets an **a**:

   _ **a** _ _ _

3. All eyes, including Sarah's, are now on the Word Wall searching for a five-letter word without the common letters **t**, **s**, or **e** and with only one **a** in the second position. The light dawns in Sarah's eyes and she quickly asks for an **l**, **u**, **g**, and **h** and wins by correctly spelling **laugh**!

4. Now Sarah goes to the board and gets to be the "teacher." She carefully draws six lines on the board:

   _ _ _ _ _ _

5. It is Jon's turn next and he asks for an **e**. There is no **e**, so the turn passes to David, who asks for an **o**. Sarah fills in the two **o**'s:

   _ _ _ **o o** _

6. David quickly asks for an **s**, **c**, **h**, and **l** and triumphantly spells the word:

   s c h o o l

7. David now takes the chalk and draws four lines on the board. The game continues until the time is up.

The Wheel is a quick-paced, fun game that will focus the students' attention on all the letters and their positions in words. The only problem is with overexuberant students who realize what the word is and say it aloud when it is not their turn. This tendency can be quickly quashed, however, if you make the rule that if the word gets said aloud before the person whose turn it is has a chance, the person whose turn it is automatically wins and becomes the teacher!

Goal Two: Decoding and Spelling Patterns

Brand Name Phonics

Here are this month's Brand Name Phonics lessons. Refer to page 16 for directions.

Lesson One
Products: **G<u>oo</u>d<u>year</u>®, <u>Ace</u>® Hardw<u>are</u>**

One-syllable words to read:
> **spear, spare, space, gear, square, stood, place, wood, rare, rear**

One-syllable words to spell:
> **fare, fear, share, near, race, trace, hood, smear, stare, pace**

Longer words to read:
> **appear, disappear, welfare, neighborhood, software, healthcare, understood, fireplace, embrace**

Longer words to spell:
> **endear, daycare, overhear, prepare, compare, plywood, aware, childhood, misplace, disgrace**

Lesson Two
Products: **B<u>a</u>nd <u>Aid</u>®, Coppert<u>one</u>®, n<u>ail</u> polish**

One-syllable words to read:
> **fail, frail, land, braid, jail, bone, bail, phone, brand, grand**

One-syllable words to spell:
> **raid, rail, trail, zone, paid, pail, snail, stone, stand, strand**

Longer words to read:
> **blackmail, hormone, mermaid, fingernail, curtail, Disneyland®, postpone, medicaid, condone, understand**

Longer words to spell:
> **retail, detail, afraid, airmail, underpaid, ozone, grandstand, backbone, expand, armband**

Lesson Three

Products: **Pam**®, **Green Giant**®, **oil**, **meat**

One-syllable words to read:
beat, screen, cheat, seen, boil, broil, slam, heat, cram, jam

One-syllable words to spell:
teen, treat, coil, seat, queen, gram, soil, spoil, scam, scram

Longer words to read:
fifteen, heartbeat, diagram, evergreen, milligram, Halloween, turmoil, defeat, monogram

Longer words to spell:
sunscreen, sixteen, repeat, retreat, recoil, program, topsoil, nineteen, preheat

Making Words

Here are February's **Making Words** lessons. (Refer to directions on page 20 and reproducibles on page 154.)

Lesson One	**Secret Word: valentines**
Letters on strip:	a e e i l n n t s v
Make:	eat, neat, live, evil, nest, sent, vent, event, eaten, alien, invest, invent, silent, listen, valentines
Sort for: related words	eat, eaten
rhyming words:	sent, vent, event, invent, silent
	nest, invest
	eat, neat
Transfer Words:	cleat, chest, spent, quest

Lesson Two   Secret Word: February

Letters on strip: a e u b f r r y

Make: by, buy, fur, ear, fear, year, rear, rare, fare, berry, ferry, furry, buyer, February

Sort for: related words   **fur, furry**
                              buy, buyer

       rhyming words: **ear, fear, year, rear**
                              rare, fare
                              berry, ferry

Transfer Words: **cherry, share, clear, merry**

Lesson Three   Secret Word: presidents

Letters on strip: e e i d n p r s s t

Make: dent, rent, ripe, ripen, dress, press, stripe, desert, dessert, pretend, present, serpent, ripened, depress, presidents

Sort for: related words: **ripe, ripen, ripened**

       rhyming words: **ripe, stripe**
                              dress, press, depress
                              dent, rent, present, serpent

Transfer Words: **mess, spent, swipe, bless**

Goal Three: Spelling Words With Two or More Possible Patterns

What Looks Right?

This month's lessons **eep/eap** and **eed/ead** patterns. The word lists are provided below. Follow the directions on page 23.

Lesson One	
sl<u>eep</u>	**ch<u>eap</u>**
deep	~~deap~~
jeep	~~jeap~~
sheep	~~sheap~~
~~leep~~	leap
sweep	~~sweap~~
steep	~~steap~~
weep	~~weap~~
creep	~~creap~~
keep	~~keap~~
seep	~~seap~~
peep	~~peap~~
~~heep~~	heap
asleep	~~asleap~~
oversleep	~~oversleap~~
beep	~~beap~~
upkeep	~~upkeap~~
upsweep	~~upsweap~~
~~reep~~	reap

Lesson Two	
f<u>eed</u>	**b<u>ead</u>**
need	~~nead~~
speed	~~spead~~
seed	~~sead~~
bleed	~~blead~~
~~leed~~	lead
reed	read
greed	~~gread~~
~~pleed~~	plead
tweed	~~twead~~
steed	~~stead~~
freed	~~fread~~
agreed	~~agread~~
exceed	~~excead~~
~~proofreed~~	proofread
indeed	~~indead~~
~~misleed~~	mislead
disagreed	~~disagread~~
seaweed	~~seawead~~
proceed	~~procead~~

Goal Four: Decoding and Spelling Polysyllabic Words

Nifty Thrifty Fifty

Here are the words for the month:

deodorize	different	employee
international	invasion	prehistoric
	signature	

These are the procedures for working with these words and their important parts:

1 Add these words to the display in your room. If you are giving students their own list, add these or duplicate this month's list (page 147).

2 Remind students that, in English, many big words are just smaller words with prefixes and suffixes added to root words. Sometimes adding these parts requires spelling or pronunciation changes. Good spellers do not memorize the spelling of every new word they meet. Rather, they notice the patterns in words. These patterns include prefixes, suffixes, and spelling changes.

3 Point to each word and have students chant it, cheerleader style, with you. After cheering for each word, help students analyze the word. Talk about meaning; determine the root, prefix, and suffix; and note any spelling changes.

deodorize	This is the word **odor** with the prefix **de** and the suffix **ize**. When you **deodorize** something, you take away the **odor**. Other words in which **de** means "to take away" include **deflate**, **defrost**, and **destabilize**.
different	**Different** is the word **differ** with the suffix **ent**.
employee	The word **employ** is shown here with the suffix **ee** meaning "person who." Other words ending in **ee** signifying a person include **nominee** and **referee**.
international	This is **nation** with the prefix **inter** and the suffix **al**. **Inter** often means "between" as in **intersection** and **intervene**. Notice how the pronunciation changes when **nation** becomes **national**.

invasion   **Invasion** is the word **invade** with the **ion** suffix. The spelling and pronunciation change is common for many words ending in **d-e**: **provide/provision, collide/collision, erode/erosion**.

prehistoric The root word **history** becomes **historic**. The suffix **pre** means "before." In actuality, nothing could happen before history, but **prehistoric** means it happened before history was written down. Thus dinosaurs are called **prehistoric** creatures. There are many other words in which the prefix **pre** means 'before," including **prefix, preview, precede**, and **predict**.

signature   The root word **sign** has the suffix **ature**. Note the change in pronunciation. Similar changes happen in related words **signal, signify**, and **significance**.

4 Once you have discussed the composition for each word, helped students see other words that work in a similar way, and cheered for each word, have students write each word. Use clues like these:

1. Number 1 is the word whose root word is **sign**.
2. Number 2 is the word whose root word is **invade**.
3. Number 3 is the word whose root word is **differ**.
4. For number 4, write the word in which **pre** means "before."
5. For number 5, write the word that begins with the prefix that means "between or among."
6. Number 6 is the word that ends in **ee** and describes a person with a job.
7. Number 7 is the word that ends in **ize**.

After students write the words, have them check their papers by once more chanting the letters aloud, underlining each letter as they say it.

5 Have students spell and write the following words contained in the new words:

odor	differ	employ
national	nation	invade
historic	history	sign

6 Next, have students spell the following words, noting how they are related to the month's new words and noting spelling changes as needed. Use each word in a sentence and talk about the meaning relationships when appropriate.

signal	**design***	**deploy**

*Note pronunciation change for s.

7 Students should be becoming skilled at using their **Nifty Thrifty Fifty** words to decode and spell other words. Here are some more to provide additional practice. Be sure to talk about meaning and spelling changes as you help students analyze these words.

disposal	**musical**	**continual**	**employer**
employment	**unemployment**	**unemployed**	**employable**
unemployable	**difference**	**consignment**	**nationality**
nationalities	**internationalize**	**internationalization**	**interdependence**
depress	**depression**	**depressive**	**deport**
deportation	**deportee**	**devalue**	**declassify**
decompose	**deform**	**deformity**	**prearrange**
resign	**resignation***	**designation***	**significant***
	significance*		

*Note pronunciation changes.

Goal Five: Applying Strategies While Reading and Writing

If possible, have students do some of their writing on a computer with a spell-check program. Have them use the feature that allows the computer to suggest a possible spelling for the misspelled word. Help them to see that the computer can search through its store of words and find similarly spelled words just as they have been learning to do. Challenge students to find big words they can decode in their reading and have them explain how the prefixes, suffixes, and roots help them with decoding and word meanings.

Guess the Covered Word

Refer to the directions on page 31. You might want to use paragraphs which describe various places being studied or which students might like to visit:

> Brazil is the **largest** country in South America. It occupies almost **half** of the continent. The **population** of Brazil is greater than that of all the other South American countries combined. If you travel in the north of Brazil, you will find the world's largest **tropical** rain forest. The mighty Amazon River flows through steamy **jungles**. The **center** of the country has fertile farmland and lush **grazing** areas. Along the Atlantic coast lie broad **white** beaches. Most of the big cities lie along this coast, as well. The interior is not well-developed and it is **sp**▮▮▮ inhabited. The language spoken in Brazil is ▮▮▮▮.

The above shows what a **Guess the Covered Word** lesson might look like after the teacher has led her students to guess the words *largest, half, population, tropical, jungles, center, grazing,* and *white.* The word *sparsely* is ready for the students to guess and uncover after seeing the beginning sound. The word *Portuguese* still needs to be guessed and uncovered.

Goal One: Learning High–Frequency, Commonly Misspelled Words

Word Wall

These are the new words for March:

3 another	2 I'm	4 its	5 it's	7 let's
10 that's	8 threw	1 through	6 very	9 with

1 Add the words to your display. If you are using different colors, you may be running out of colors for those troublesome, omnipresent "w" and "t" words. Repeat colors if needed but be sure to put homophones on different colors. Attach clues with "it is" next to **it's** and a picture of a ball next to **threw**. If you are also using the Portable Word Walls, give students a new sheet to which the new words (and clues) have been added (reproducible, page 139).

2 Focus student attention on each word and have students chant it, cheerleader style, with you. Before cheering for each word, point out helpful clues and illogicalities!

another	Students should realize this is a compound word made up of **an** and **other**.
its, it's; threw, through	By now, students should not need any explanation of how the clues you are attaching help them know which word to use. Help them use **its**, **it's**, **threw**, and **through** in sentences. There is no logic to **through** being spelled like **enough**!
I'm, let's, that's	Students should figure out that these are contractions for **I am**, **let us**, and **that is**. Make sure students notice the capital **I** in **I'm**. **Remember to click and gesture for the apostrophe when cheering.**
very	Most words rhyming with **very** have two **r**'s (**berry**, **merry**, etc.), but **very** is spelled just like the **every** students have been spelling in **everyone**, **everybody**, and **everything**.
with	This is a logical word but still often misspelled.

3 Use writing clues to have students write each word:

1. Number 1 is a four-letter w word that fits in this sentence: Do you want fries _____ that?

2. Number 2 is a contraction that always needs a capital letter.

3. For number 3, write the seven-letter compound word that rhymes with **brother**.

4. Write the five-letter word that tells something you did with a ball.

5. For number 5, write the other word that is pronounced just like the word you wrote for 4.

6. This word is a contraction for **let us**.

7. This word is a contraction for **that is**.

8. This word is a contraction for **it is**.

9. Write the other word that is pronounced just like the word you wrote for number 8.

10. Write the only word on the wall that begins with a **v**.

After students write the ten words, have them check their papers by once more chanting the letters aloud, underlining each letter as they say it.

4 Throughout the month, use down time to review words by cheering, writing, and by playing a few rounds of **Be a Mind Reader** or **The Wheel**. (Directions for **Be a Mind Reader** are on page 50. Directions for **The Wheel** can be found on page 87.) Don't give up on writing WW when needed, although the need for that should be lessening. You—and your students—should be reaping the rewards of your determination!

Goal Two: Learning One– and Two–Syllable Words That Follow a Pattern, but Are Used Less Frequently

Brand Name Phonics

By now, the students have had lots of practice with how words they know can help them spell and read lots of other words. Duplicate the list on page 99, which contains all the patterns and the words from which they came. Give students the list and let them work in teams to see how many words they can spell which follow each pattern. Have them brainstorm words and then check the spellings in a dictionary if they are unsure of which pattern to use. This is particularly important when rhymes such as **air/are**, **ane/ain**, **ear/eer**, and **ean/een** have two different spelling patterns. Just as in lessons, encourage students to include words whose last syllable rhymes with the key word. You may want to cut along the lines to divide the list according to vowels (with **o** and **u** combined) and do the activity across four different days.

Brand Name Phonics Word Patterns

ace	Ace Hardware®
ack	Snack Pack®
ade	lemonade
aid	Band Aid®, Kool Aid®
ail	nail polish
ain	White Rain®
air	hair spray
ake	Shake 'n' Bake®
ale	ginger ale
all	all®
am	Pam®
an	Ban®
and	Band Aid®
ane	candy cane
ank	— Bank
ap	ginger snap
ape	grape
are	Ace Hardware®
art	Wal-Mart®
at	fat free, Kit Kat®
ate	Colgate®
ay	hair spray, Ocean Spray®

each	Reach®
eam	ice cream
ean	jelly bean
ear	Good Year®
eat	Wheat Thins®, meat
ee	fat free
eed	Speed Stick®
een	Green Giant®
eer	Cheer®
eet	Sweet 'n' Low®
ell	Taco Bell®
est	Crest®
ew	Mountain Dew®

ice	ice cream
ick	Speed Stick®
ide	Tide®
ight	Right Guard®
im	Slim Jim®
ime	lemon-lime®
in	Wheat Thins®
ine	Pine Sol®
ing	Burger King®
ip	Cool Whip®
ipe	Fudge Stripes®
ish	Gold Fish®
it	Kit Kat®
ite	Sprite®, White Rain®

og	Dog Chow®
oke	Diet Coke®
oil	oil
old	Bold®
one	Coppertone®
ood	Good Year®
ool	Cool Whip®, Kool Aid®
oot	root beer
op	popcorn
ope	Scope®
ore	Dollar Store
orn	popcorn
ound	Mounds®
out	Shout®
ow	Dog Chow®
ow	Ivory Snow®, Sweet 'n' Low®
oy	Almond Joy®

un	Capri Sun®
ut	Pizza Hut®

Making Words

Here are the **Making Words** lessons for March. Refer to the directions on page 20 and reproducibles on page 155.

Lesson One	**Secret Word: newspaper**
Letters on strip:	a e e n p p r s w
Make:	see, sea, new, saw, paw, raw, rap, wrap, weep, sweep, erase, renew, paper, answer, newspaper
Sort for: related words	new, renew, newspaper
rhyming words:	saw, raw, paw weep, sweep
Transfer Words:	claw, steep, sheep, straw

Lesson Two	**Secret Word: basketball**
Letters on strip:	a a e b b k l l s t
Make:	tall, ball, bell, sell, east, last, talk, stalk, stall, blast, beast, table, stable, baseball, basketball
Sort for: rhyming words:	tall, ball, stall, baseball, basketball bell, sell east, beast talk, stalk last, blast table, stable
Transfer Words:	cable, least, chalk, past

Lesson Three	**Secret Word: tournament**
Letters on strip:	a e o u m n n r t t

Make: out, rot, trot, name, tame, team, menu, trout, mount, amount, nature, mature, torment, ornament, tournament

Sort for:

words ending in **ture**:	nature, mature
words ending in **ment**:	torment, ornament, tournament
rhyming words:	out, trout rot, trot name, tame

Transfer Words: scout, flame, shame, clot

Goal Three: Spelling Words With Two or More Patterns

What Looks Right?

Now that students understand that some rhymes have two common spelling patterns, they are ready to realize that a few rhymes have three common spelling patterns. These lessons will help students use the **oal/ole/oll** and **oan/one/own** patterns. Use the word lists below and on the following page, and the directions on page 23.

Lesson One

goal	hole	toll
coal	cole	~~coll~~
~~moal~~	mole	~~moll~~
~~stoal~~	stole	~~stoll~~
~~poal~~	pole	poll
~~roal~~	role	roll
~~troal~~	~~trole~~	troll
~~stroal~~	~~strole~~	stroll
~~scroal~~	~~scrole~~	scroll
foal	~~fole~~	~~foll~~
~~doal~~	dole	~~doll~~
charcoal	~~charcole~~	~~charcoll~~
~~casseroal~~	casserole	~~casseroll~~
~~foxhoal~~	foxhole	~~foxholl~~
~~tadpoal~~	tadpole	~~tadpoll~~
~~payroal~~	~~payrole~~	payroll
~~enroal~~	~~enrole~~	enroll
~~steamroal~~	~~steamrole~~	steamroll

Lesson Two

moan	phone	own
~~boan~~	bone	~~bown~~
~~zoan~~	zone	~~zown~~
~~stoan~~	stone	~~stown~~
~~floan~~	~~flone~~	flown
~~bloan~~	~~blone~~	blown*
~~toan~~	tone	~~town~~ *
moan	~~mone~~	~~mown~~ *
groan	~~grone~~	grown*
~~throan~~	throne	thrown*
~~shoan~~	~~shone~~	shown*
loan	lone	~~lown~~
~~cloan~~	clone	~~clown~~ *
~~droan~~	drone	~~drown~~ *
~~aloan~~	alone	~~alown~~
~~Yellowstoan~~	Yellowstone	~~Yellowstown~~
~~microphoan~~	microphone	~~microphown~~
~~hormoan~~	hormone	~~hormown~~
~~ozoan~~	ozone	~~ozown~~
~~condoan~~	condone	~~condown~~
~~disoan~~	~~disone~~	disown
~~tromboan~~	trombone	~~trombown~~
~~tombstoan~~	tombstone	~~tombstown~~

*At the end of the lesson, point out that some **o-w-n** words (**shown**, **grown**, etc.) are the past tenses of other **o-w** words. Also point out that **town**, **clown**, and **drown** are **o-w-n** words that follow the other **o-w-n** pronunciation pattern. There are just a few spelling patterns that have two common pronunciations, including **o-w-n**, **o-w**, and **e-a-r**.

Goal Four: Decoding and Spelling Polysyllabic Words

Nifty Thrifty Fifty

Below are the final words to complete the **Nifty Thrifty Fifty** list. Reproducibles for this month's words can be found on page 148.

antifreeze	forecast	midnight
overpower	semifinal	supermarket
	underweight	

 Add these words to your list, then talk about each one and cheer for it:

antifreeze	This is the word **freeze** with the prefix **anti** meaning "against." Other words in which **anti** means against include **antibody**, **antibiotic**, and **antihistamine**.
forecast	This is the word **cast** with the prefix **fore**, meaning "before" or "in front of." Other words in which **fore** has this meaning include **forehead**, **foresight, foreshadow**, and **forewarn**.
midnight	Here the word **night** has the prefix **mid**, meaning "middle." Other words in which **mid** has this meaning include **midpoint**, **midlife**, **midyear**, and **midair**.
overpower	This is the word **power** with the prefix **over**, meaning "more than" or "too much." Other words in which **over** has this meaning include **overcharge**, **overflow**, **overjoyed**, and **overload**.
semifinal	**Semifinal** is the word **final** with the prefix **semi**, meaning "half." Other words in which **semi** has this meaning include **semicolon**, **semiannual**, **semisweet**, and **semiconductor**.
supermarket	This is the word **market** with the prefix **super**, meaning "really big." Other words in which **super** has this meaning include **superpower**, **supertanker**, **supersaver**, and **superman**.
underweight	Here is the word **weight** with the prefix **under**, meaning "below." Other words in which **under** has this meaning include **underclass**, **underground, undertow**, and **underprivileged**.

2 Once you have discussed the composition for each word, helped students see other words that work in a similar way, and cheered for each word, have students write each word. Here are some suggested clues:

1. Number 1 is the opposite of **overweight**.

2. Number 2 is the word for telling what tomorrow's weather will be.

3. Number 3 is the hour at which one day ends and another begins.

4. For number 4, write the word in which **semi** means "half."

5. For number 5, write the word in which **anti** means "against."

6. Number 6 is the word in which **super** means "really big."

7. Number 7 is the word that contains the root word **power**.

After students write the words, have them check their papers by once more chanting the letters aloud, underlining each as they say it.

3 Have students spell and write the following words contained in the new words:

over	under	super	freeze	cast
night	power	final	market	weight

4 Here are some words students can spell by combining parts of the new words:

overnight	overweight	overcast

5 Here are some words students should be able to spell by using parts of all fifty words:

freezer	freezing	freezable	subfreezing	underclass
overexpose	underexpose	superimpose	undercover	forecaster
forecasting	miscast	antidepressant	overture	deodorant
empower	empowerment	powerful	powerfully	powerfulness
powerless	powerlessly	powerlessness	superpower	finalize
finalizing	finalization	weighty	weightier	weightiest
weightless	undervalue	friendlier	friendliest	friendliness
unfriendliness	unpleasantness	historical	historically	expressive
impressive	repressive	invasive	noninvasive	invasiveness
hopefully	hopelessly	predispose	predisposition	courageous*

*The **e** is not dropped because the sound of **g** would change.

Be a Mind Reader

Now that students have learned all 50 **Nifty Thrifty Fifty** words, they might enjoy playing **Be a Mind Reader** with them. For **Be a Mind Reader**, think of a word and give students five clues which narrow to only one possible word. Everyone should get it by the last clue, but did anyone "read your mind" and get it on an earlier clue? Have students number their papers from 1 to 5 and give five clues such as these (for the word *international*):

1. *"It's one of our **Nifty Thrifty Fifty** words."* (Students hate this but often someone guesses the word and then they love it!) Have them write the word they think you mean next to number 1.

2. *"It has ten or more letters."* (This narrows it down considerably!) If a student has a ten or more letter word for number 1, he would write it again. If not, he needs to choose and write a different word with ten or more letters.

3. *"It begins with the letter **i**."* (This narrows it to only five words.)

4. *"It contains an **r**."* (**Impossible** and **independence** are eliminated.)

5. *"It begins with the prefix **inter**."*

By now, everyone should have it, but find out who had it earlier and express amazement that they "read your mind!"

Here's another example:

1. It's one of our **Nifty Thrifty Fifty** words.

2. It begins with a **c**.

3. It begins with **com**.

4. It is not a person.

5. To spell it, you have to change the **y** to **i** and add **es**.

(communities)

Goal Five: Applying Strategies While Reading and Writing

Guess the Covered Word helps students cross check meaning, word length, and all the beginning letters up to the vowel to figure out words. To do a **Guess the Covered Word** activity, write sentences or a paragraph related to something students are studying or a topic of general interest. Select one word per sentence which begins with a consonant letter and cover that word with two torn sticky notes, with the first part covering all the beginning consonant letters up to the vowel. Read each sentence and have students make guesses about the missing word without any letters revealed. Write down the guesses. Remove the sticky note that covers the beginning letter(s). Erase any guesses which are no longer possible and have students make additional guesses for the word that both make sense and have the right beginning letters. When the students cannot think of any more words that meet the criteria, reveal the rest of the word and see if the correct word was guessed.

Guess the Covered Word

In many places, March is a windy month, perfect for flying kites!

There are **hundreds** of different kinds of kites. Most kites are made of paper or cloth mounted on a **frame**, to which a line is attached. The forces of lift, drag, and **gravity** combine to keep a kite in the air. A kite's ability to fly in the wind depends upon its **construction** and the way its **line** is attached. Some kites can fly with only a light **breeze**. Others **require** wind speeds of more than ten miles per hour. Kites are the oldest **f[____]** of aircraft. They originated in **[____]** about 3,000 years ago.

The paragraph above shows what a **Guess the Covered Word** lesson might look like after the teacher has led her students to guess the words *hundreds, frame, gravity, construction, line, breeze,* and *require*. The word *form* is ready for the students to guess and uncover after seeing the beginning sound. The word *China* still needs to be guessed and uncovered.

Goal One: Learning High–Frequency, Commonly Misspelled Words

Word Wall

These are the new words for April:

almost	also	always	probably	we're
wear	where	wouldn't	your	you're

1 Add the words to your display. If you are using different colors, you may be running out of colors for those troublesome, omnipresent "w" and "t" words. Repeat colors if needed but be sure to put homophones on different colors. Attach clues with "you are" next to **you're**, "we are" next to **we're**, and a picture of a hat next to **wear**. If you are also using the Portable Word Walls, give students a new sheet to which the new words (and clues) have been added (reproducible, page 140).

2 Focus student attention on each word and have students chant it, cheerleader style, with you. Before "cheering" for each word, point out helpful clues and illogicalities!

almost, also, always	All of these are words in which the first syllable could logically be spelled **a-l-l**.
probably	This is another word like **really** and **usually** that ends in **ly**. Often misspelled because it is often pronounced "probly."
your, you're; we're, wear, where	Clues should help determine which one to use when writing; all are illogical spellings which don't follow the patterns.
wouldn't	This is the contraction for **would not**. **Would** is spelled like **could** and **should**. Students should also be able to spell **couldn't** and **shouldn't**.

3 Use writing clues to have students write each word:

1. Number 1 is a word that begins with **al** and fits in this sentence: Why does it _____ rain on football nights?

2. Number 2 is a word that begins with **al** and fits in this sentence: That car is fast, and a good buy, _____.

3. Number 3 is a word that begins with **al** and fits in this sentence: I didn't finish my home-work but I _____ did.

4. Write the four-letter word that begins with **y**.

5. For number 5, write the contraction that is pronounced just like the word you wrote for number 4.

6. This word is a contraction for **would not**.

7. This word is a contraction for **we are**.

8. This word begins with a **w** and fits in this sentence: I have nothing to _____.

9. Write the other word that is pronounced just like the word you wrote for number 8.

10. Write the eight-letter word that begins with **p**.

After students write the ten words, have them check their papers by once more chanting the letters aloud, underlining each letter as they say it.

4 Continue to review words as the year comes to a close. In addition to the words on the wall, you may want to have students learn other words spelled like the Word Wall words, including these:

someone	would	should	shouldn't	couldn't
anybody	anything	yourself	himself	herself

Goal Two: Learning One– and Two–Syllable Words That Follow a Pattern, but Are Used Less Frequently

Brand Name Phonics

Students should now be quite adept at using words they can spell to help them decode and spell lots of other words. **The final step in making them independent decoders is to help them see that all the words they can spell—not just the brand names—are available to them as decoding and spelling helps.** To demonstrate this, you might divide the class into teams which can accumulate points by using words they know to figure out how to read and spell other words. Here are the steps for this team decoding/spelling challenge:

1 Seat the team members closely together so that they can quietly consult on each word. Provide them with paper on which to write words they know that will help them.

2 For the decoding words, show a word to everyone and give teams one minute to consult and come up with one or more words that are spelled like and rhyme with the word you have shown. At the end of one minute, ask the team whose turn it is to read and spell one known word and decode the shown word. If they are correct, give them two points—one point for having a usable known word and one point for successfully decoding the shown word.

3 Now, go to the other teams and see if they can tell you another word—not the one mentioned by the first team—which would also work. Give them one point for having another usable word. The reason for this step is to show students that you often have lots of words—not just one "magic" word—that will help you.

4 Continue to show one-syllable words which have several rhyming words which would help them. Make your words fairly uncommon words, but words your students probably would have heard. Here are some possibilities to get you started:

brace	blade	shrug	slope	chore	thorn	shock	frown
drool	swoop	screen	vast	chart	creek	slob	wrong

5 Next, use the same procedure to have students decode some words in which the last syllable rhymes with words they know. Give them three points for these words—one for finding a matching rhyming word for the last syllable, one for decoding the last syllable, and one for figuring out the whole word. Just as with one-syllable words, go to other teams for other words that will work and give them one point. Here are some possibilities:

toothpicks	shampoo	distress	defeat	reveal	Yankee
mustang	invade	compute	excuse	platform	explore
termite	hybrid	describe	regret	success	conceal

6 Spelling, of course, is harder because some words have two rhyming patterns and you have to know which one looks right. Here are some words, however, which only have one possibility. Say each word. Let teams confer to figure out a rhyming word and how to spell the word you said. Award points as before, including one point to other teams who come up with other possibilities:

blip	scold	stump	spy	slick	chest	trend	prank
grit	prong	spunk	blush	skin	swell	shack	grave

7 Finally, here are some three-point words which can't reasonably be spelled any other way:

aircraft	program	expand	whiplash	contrast
engrave	suspend	frequent	conquest	lipstick
employ	describe	format	admit	forbid

Making Words

Here are three **Making Words** Lessons for April. Refer to the directions on page 20 and reproducibles on page 156).

Lesson One

Letters on strip:

Secret Word: Internet

e e i n n r t t

Make: in, tin, inn, net, ten, teen, tent, rent, inner, enter, entire, intent, intern, Internet

Sort for: related words: in, inner

rhyming words: in, tin
tent, rent, intent

Transfer Words: bent, vent, thin, chin

Lesson Two

Letters on strip:

Secret Word: telephone

e e e o h l n p t

Make: ten, hen, eel, heel, open, tone, lone, pole, hole, hope, elope, hotel, tepee, telephone

Sort for: rhyming words: ten, hen
tone, lone, telephone
pole, hole
hope, elope

Transfer Words: scope, mole, when, bone

Lesson Three

Letters on strip:

Secret Word: restaurant

a a e u n r r s t t

Make: sue, ant, aunt, nest, true, rant, rust, trust, arena, rerun, state, statue, return, arrest, restaurant

Sort for: words beginning with **re**:   rerun, return

rhyming words: sue, true, statue
ant, rant
rust, trust
nest, arrest

Transfer Words: crust, clue, slant, west

Goal Three: Spelling Words With Two or More Patterns

What Looks Right?

Here are word lists for two more lessons for rhymes have three common spelling patterns. Refer to directions on page 23.

Lesson One

<u>air</u>	<u>care</u>	<u>wear</u>
~~scair~~	scare	~~scear~~
~~squair~~	square	~~squear~~
chair	~~chare~~	~~chear~~
~~rair~~	rare	~~rear~~ *
~~spair~~	spare	~~spear~~ *
~~swair~~	~~sware~~	swear
pair	pare	pear
hair	hare	~~hear~~ *
~~bair~~	bare	bear
fair	fare	~~fear~~ *
flair	flare	~~flear~~
~~glair~~	glare	~~glear~~
~~blair~~	blare	~~blear~~
~~awair~~	aware	~~awear~~
~~compair~~	compare	~~compear~~
~~underwair~~	~~underware~~	underwear
wheelchair	~~wheelchare~~	~~wheelchear~~
repair	~~repare~~	~~repear~~
~~prepair~~	prepare	~~prepear~~
unfair	~~unfare~~	~~unfear~~

---

*Help students to realize that these words are words they know and go with the **ear/near** rhyming pattern. The pattern **e-a-r** has two common pronunciations. Also point out high-frequency words **where**, **there**, and **their**, which rhyme with these but which aren't spelled according to any pattern. Remind students that many commonly used words don't follow the usual patterns.

Lesson Two

true	new	zoo
~~chue~~	chew	~~choo~~
~~drue~~	drew	~~droo~~
glue	~~glew~~	~~gloo~~
~~bue~~	~~bew~~	boo
~~grue~~	grew	~~groo~~
~~stue~~	stew	~~stoo~~
~~brue~~	brew	~~broo~~
blue	blew	~~bloo~~
due	dew	~~doo~~
~~scrue~~	screw	~~scroo~~
sue	~~sew~~	~~soo~~
~~crue~~	crew	~~croo~~
~~mue~~	mew	moo
~~cashue~~	cashew	~~cashoo~~
~~renue~~	renew	~~renoo~~
avenue	~~avenew~~	~~avenoo~~
revenue	~~revenew~~	~~revenoo~~
~~shampue~~	~~shampew~~	shampoo
~~outgrue~~	outgrew	~~outgroo~~
~~bambue~~	~~bambew~~	bamboo
~~kangarue~~	~~kangarew~~	kangaroo
overdue	~~overdew~~	~~overdoo~~
pursue	~~pursew~~	~~pursoo~~

At the end of the lesson, point out high-frequency words **to**, **do**, **who**, **shoe**, **two**, and **through**, which rhyme with the above words but which aren't spelled according to any pattern. Remind students that many commonly-used words don't follow the usual patterns.

Goal Four: Decoding and Spelling Polysyllabic Words

Students should now be able to spell and analyze the parts of all 50 words on the **Nifty Thrifty Fifty** list. This month, focus specifically on the prefixes, suffixes, and spelling changes students have learned, helping them consolidate meanings for these. Also, help students see that sometimes word parts are not prefixes or suffixes that change the meaning of the word, but just chunks that help them decode and spell the words. Lead students to create a chart showing examples of words in which the prefix meaning is evident and in which the prefix meaning is not evident. Provide other examples for suffixes and endings and focus on how the word changes in spelling and use.

Prefixes

Duplicate the Prefix Chart on pages 116-117 or have students make their own in their notebooks. Talk with students about each prefix and its meaning. Then, have students use the dictionary to find two more examples of words in which the prefix has that meaning as well as two words in which it does not. (For some prefixes, such as **non**, **fore**, **over**, and **under**, there are not two common words in which the prefix does not function as a meaning unit.)

The "Unpeelable" Prefixes

In addition to the prefixes on the chart, which leave independent words when taken off, **there are other common prefixes which do not leave recognizable words when they are "peeled off."** The prefixes **con/com**, **ex**, **em**, and **per** do add meanings to words, but you have to have a rather advanced understanding of Latin and Greek roots to see the meaning relationships. It is probably best to just help students see how these are predictable spelling and pronunciation chunks rather than try to show students how to analyze these words for meaning clues. Here are some examples of these "unpeelable" prefixes:

Unpeelable Prefix	Nifty Word	Other Examples
com/con	community/ies	competition, communism
	composer	computer, compassion
	continuous	construction, conclusion
	conversation	constitution, concrete
em	employee	embassy, embryo
ex	expensive	excitement, explain
per	performance	permanent, personality

Prefix Chart

Prefix	Meaning	Meaning Chunk	Spelling/Pronunciation Chunk
re	back	replacement	refrigerator
re	again	rearrange	reward
un	opposite	unfriendly, unfinished unpleasant	uncle
in (im, ir, il)	opposite	independence	incident
		impossible	imagine
		irresponsible	irritate
		illegal	illustrate
in (im)	in	invasion	instant
		impression	immense
dis	opposite	dishonest, discovery	distress
non	opposite	nonliving	—
en	in	encourage	entire

mis	bad, wrong	misunderstand	miscellaneous
		_____	_____
pre	before	prehistoric	present
		_____	_____
inter	between	international	interesting
		_____	_____
de	opposite/ take away	deodorize	delight
		_____	_____
sub	under	submarine	subsist
		_____	_____
fore	before/ in front of	forecast	—
		_____	
trans	across	transportation	—
		_____	
super	really big	supermarkets	superintendent
		_____	_____
semi	half	semifinal	seminar
		_____	_____
mid	middle	midnight	midget
		_____	_____
over	too much	overpower	—
		_____	
under	below	underweight	understand
		_____	
anti	against	antifreeze	—
		_____	_____
		_____	_____

Suffixes, Endings, and Spelling Changes

Suffix/Ending	Nifty Word	Other Examples
s/es	supermarkets	musicians, signatures
(y-i)	communities	discoveries, countries
ed/ing	unfinished	performed, misunderstanding
(drop e)	nonliving	replaced, continuing
(double m)	swimming	forgetting, batted
er/est	richest	smarter, bigger
(y-i)	prettier	craziest, happier
en (double t)	forgotten	written, bitten
less	hopeless	careless, penniless
ful (y-i)	beautiful	successful, pitiful
able (drop e)	valuable	portable, incurable
ible	irresponsible	reversible, horrible (horror)
tion	transportation	imagination, solution (solve)
	conversation	graduation, investigation
sion	invasion	explosion, decision (decide)
	impression	expression, permission (permit)
ly	unfriendly	hopelessly, happily
er	composer	reporter, robber
or	governor	dictator, juror
ee	employee	referee, trainee
ian	musician	magician, beautician
ance	performance	attendance, ignorance
ence	independence	conference, persistence
ment	encouragement	punishment, involvement
	replacement	government, refreshment
ness (y-i)	happiness	goodness, business
y	discovery	jealousy, pregnancy
ity	electricity	popularity, possibility
ant	unpleasant	tolerant, dominant
ent	different	confident, excellent
al	international	political, racial
ive	expensive	inconclusive, competitive
ous	continuous	humorous, ambitious
ic	prehistoric	scenic, specific (specify)
ify	classify	beautify, identify
ize	deodorize	modernize, standardize
ture	signature	creature, fracture

118

For suffixes and endings, focus not on a meaning change but on a change in how and where the word fits into a sentence. Discuss how the spelling of the root word often determines the spelling of the suffix. Use words from the **Nifty Thrifty Fifty** list to help students transfer to other words. Talk about meaning and spelling, and discuss how each word could be used in a sentence.

Remember that, in order to use these words to decode, spell, and access meaning for lots of other big words, students need plenty of practice. They need to be able to automatically, correctly, and fluently spell these words. If students enjoyed **Be a Mind Reader** last month, continue to do a few rounds when you have some minutes to "sponge" up (see directions, page 50).

The Wheel

To play **The Wheel**, draw blanks on the board to represent the letters in a **Nifty Thrifty Fifty** word. Have students draw this many blanks on their papers. Go around the class, letting students ask for letters. If the letter is there, write it in the appropriate blank and let that student ask again. A student can continue asking until she asks for a letter that is not in the word. Then, go on to the next student. The winner is the first person to spell the whole word correctly, and the winner becomes the "teacher" for the next lesson. Here is an example:

---

1. The teacher draws nine blanks on the board and says, "Our first word has nine letters. Al, guess a letter."

2. Al asks for a **t**. There is no **t**, so the teacher moves on to David, who asks for an **r**. There is no **r** either. Nor is there an **o**, for which Carol asks. Next, Jon asks for and gets an **a**:

   _ _ _ _ _ _ _ **a** _

3. All eyes, including Jon's, are now looking at the **Nifty Thrifty Fifty** words, searching for a nine-letter word without the common letters **t**, **r**, or **o** and with only one **a** in the next-to-last position. The light dawns in Jon's eyes and he quickly asks for an **s**, **e**, **m**, **i**, **f**, **n**, and **l** and wins by correctly spelling **semifinal**!

4. Now Jon goes to the board and gets to be the "teacher." He carefully draws ten lines on the board:

   _ _ _ _ _ _ _ _ _ _

5. It is Willy's turn next and he asks for an **o**. There is no **o**. Jim asks for a **u**. Jon fills in the one **u**:

   u _ _ _ _ _ _ _ _ _

6. Jim then asks for an **n**:

   u n _ _ _ _ _ _ **n** _

7. Jim then asks for a **p**, **l**, **e**, **a**, **s**, and **t** and spells the word **unpleasant**. Jim now takes the chalk and draws ten lines on the board. The game continues until the time is up.

The Wheel is a quick-paced, fun game that will focus the students' attention on all the letters and their positions in words. The only problem is with overexuberant students who realize what the word is and say it aloud when it is not their turn. This tendency can be quickly quashed, however, if you make the rule that if the word gets said aloud before the person whose turn it is has a chance, the person whose turn it is automatically wins and becomes the "teacher"!

Goal Five: Applying Strategies While Reading and Writing

Continue your reminders to students as they begin reading and writing assignments. When you are reading or editing with them, coach them to use strategies as needed by saying things like these:

"One of our **Nifty Thrifty Fifty** words ends like that."

"Do you know a word that has the **a-w-k** spelling pattern?"

"**S-t-r-o-a-k** is a possible way to spell this word, but there is another rhyming pattern. Can you think of other words that rhyme with **stroke** and have a different spelling pattern?"

"You spelled **creation** with **s-h-u-n** at the end. It sounds like it should be **s-h-u-n**, but how are big words that sound like that at the end actually spelled?"

Guess the Covered Word

It's spring and time to notice again all the small wonders of the world, including butterflies! (Refer to the directions for **Guess the Covered Word** on page 31.)

Butterflies live in almost all the **countries** of the world. Tropical rain forests have the greatest number of **different** kinds of butterflies. Butterflies begin life as tiny eggs and **hatch** into caterpillars. In the **winter** , some butterflies travel over 2,000 miles from Canada to California, **Florida** , or **Mexico** . Here they rest and **conserve** energy for their return flight in the **spring** . Other **species** of butterflies survive the winter by hibernating in a **sh**▒▒▒ place. Many people ▒▒▒ that butterflies are the most beautiful insect.

The above shows what a **Guess the Covered Word** lesson might look like after the teacher has led her students to guess the words *countries, different, hatch, winter, Florida, Mexico, conserve, spring,* and *species*. The word *sheltered* is ready for the students to guess and uncover after seeing the beginning sound. The word *believe* still needs to be guessed and uncovered.

Goal One: Learning High–Frequency, Commonly Misspelled Words

Word Wall

These are the final ten words to be added:

anyone	getting	terrible	thought	trouble
were	weather	whether	whole	hole

1 Add the words to your display. (The "Portable Word Wall" on page 141 shows what your Word Wall should look like after the May/June words have been added.) If you are using different colors, you may be running out of colors for those "w" and "t" words. Repeat colors if needed but be sure to put homophones on different colors. Attach clues such as a picture of some bad weather to **weather** and a picture of a donut hole to **hole**. If you are also using the Portable Word Walls, give students a new sheet to which the new words (and clues) have been added (reproducible, page 141).

2 Focus student attention on each word and have students chant it, cheerleader style, with you. Before cheering for each word, point out helpful clues and illogicalities!

anyone	This is a compound word with **any** and **one**.
getting	Double the **t** before adding **ing**. This is spelled like **betting** and **petting**, although often pronounced like **sitting** and **spitting**.
terrible	This is a logical word but often misspelled with only one **r** or with an **el** at the end.
thought	This is an illogical spelling but the same pattern is used in other words including **ought**, **bought**, and **brought**.
trouble	Here is another illogical spelling, but the same pattern used in the word **double**.
were	**Were** is another **w** word with an illogical spelling.
weather, whether; hole, whole	Clues should help determine which one to use when writing.

3 Use writing clues to have students write each word:

1. Number 1 is a four-letter **w** word that fits in this sentence: Where _____ you last night?

2. Number 2 is a seven-letter word that begins with **t** and ends with **le.**

3. Number 3 is an eight-letter word that begins with **t** and ends with **le.**

4. Write the compound word that begins with **any.**

5. For number 5, write the only **g** word on the wall.

6. Write the word that begins with **th** and rhymes with **ought** and **bought.**

7. This word begins with **wh** and fits in this sentence: I can't believe I ate the _____ thing.

8. Write the other word that is pronounced just like the word you wrote for number 7.

9. Write the **w** word that fits in this sentence: I can't decide _____ or not I should go.

10. Write the other word that is pronounced just like the word you wrote for number 9.

After students write the ten words, have them check their papers by once more chanting the letters aloud, underlining each letter as they say it.

As the year comes to a close, your students should be much better spellers, not just of these words but of lots of other words. **The Word Wall activities you have done should have focused students' attention on the spelling of words. Students should realize that most— but not all—words follow patterns. A fringe benefit of the Word Wall activities you have done should be students' heightened sensitivity to new words they meet. They should be deciding for themselves if a new word follows a pattern and can thus be spelled logically, or if there is something illogical in the word.**

Goal Two: Learning One– and Two–Syllable Words That Follow a Pattern, but Are Used Less Frequently

Hink Pinks

What do you call the noise that a hunting dog makes? a person who steals your bedtime reading material? the place where an "odiferous" animal sleeps? an evil female ruler? Make the answers to these riddles rhyme and you have created **Hink Pinks**. To create **Hink Pinks**, begin with lots of rhyming words—including those with different spelling patterns. Then, choose two—such as **hound sound**, **book crook**, **skunk bunk**, or **mean queen**—and come up with the question. A fun way to review the concept of the rhyme-spelling connection in this final month of school is to let students work in teams to create their own **Hink Pinks**. Each team should come up with five they think are terrific and then ask them as riddles to the other teams in the classroom.

> **For a challenge, you might ask each team to try to think of one "Hinky Pinky" using two-syllable rhyming words. Remind them that there is to be no "hanky panky" in their teams, but that it is fine if they're in a "busy tizzy." Tell them that you expect all their Hinky Pinky riddles to be "super duper!"**

Making Words

Here are three **Making Words** lessons for this month. Refer to the directions on page 20 and reproducibles on page 157.

Lesson One	**Secret Word: vacations**
Letters on strip:	a a i o c n s t v
Make:	not, cot, cat, scat, cast, vast, into, coin, cost, coast, canvas, casino, vacant, actions, vacations
Sort for: words ending in **tions**:	actions, vacations
rhyming words:	not, cot cat, scat cast, vast
Transfer Words:	blast, shot, brat, fast

Lesson Two

Secret Word: adventures

Letters on strip: a e e u d n r s t v

Make: due, dune, tune, save, Dave, east, dent, vent, event, avenue, nature, veteran, eastern, dentures, adventures

Sort for: related words: east, eastern

words ending in **ture**: nature, denture, adventure

rhyming words: due, avenue
save, Dave
dune, tune
dent, vent, event

Transfer Words: grave, glue, prune, spent

Lesson Three

Secret Word: graduate

Letters on strip: a a e u d g r t

Make: age, due, true, tear, gear, area, rage, rate, date, gate, grate, great, argue, guard, graduate

Sort for: rhyming words: age, rage
tear, gear
rate, date, gate, grate, graduate
due, true, argue

Transfer Words: crate, smear, stage, blue

Goal Three: Spelling Words With Two or More Patterns

What Looks Right?

For the final lessons, work with spelling patterns which only occur in longer words but which are very common: **tion/sion** and **le/el/al**. Use the word lists below and on the following page. Refer to page 23 for directions.

Lesson One	
mo<u>tion</u>	**pen<u>sion</u>**
action	~~acsion~~
station	~~stasion~~
~~mantion~~	mansion
mention	~~mension~~
lotion	~~losion~~
nation	~~nasion~~
~~tention~~	tension
attention	~~attension~~
~~extention~~	extension
~~expantion~~	expansion
multiplication	~~multiplicasion~~
~~divition~~	division
~~televition~~	television
vacation	~~vacasion~~
~~collition~~	collision

Looks **Right**

Looks **Right**

Lesson Two

people	model	animal
~~travle~~	travel	~~traval~~
little	~~littel~~	~~littal~~
~~channle~~	channel	~~channal~~
~~locle~~	~~locel~~	local
~~equle~~	~~equel~~	equal
~~loyle~~	~~loyel~~	loyal
settle	~~settel~~	~~settal~~
poodle	~~poodel~~	~~poodal~~
bubble	~~bubbel~~	~~bubbal~~
~~tunnle~~	tunnel	~~tunnal~~
~~normle~~	~~normel~~	normal
~~generle~~	~~generel~~	general
possible	~~possibel~~	~~possibal~~
invisible	~~invisibel~~	~~invisibal~~
principle	~~principel~~	principal

Goal Four: Decoding and Spelling Polysyllabic Words

It's the end of the year and time to consolidate the **Nifty Thrifty Fifty** list and help students see how the patterns they know in big words will help them spell lots of other words. If your students enjoy playing **Be a Mind Reader** and **The Wheel,** continue to sponge up time with these activities (see directions on pages 50 and 87). To give students practice using the parts of lots of words, play **Mystery Word Match**.

Mystery Word Match

Mystery Word Match is a game similar to "Twenty Questions" in which students try to guess a mystery word which has parts like two or three clue words. To play, divide the students into two teams. Write each sentence and clue words on the board. The mystery word is worth ten points. Read the sentence, saying "blank" for the mystery word. Pronounce the clue words and have the students pronounce them. Students ask questions such as, "Does the mystery word begin like (one of the clue words)? End like . . .? Have a middle like . . . ?" With each "no" answer to a question, the turn shifts to the other team and a point is subtracted. Here is an example:

1. The teacher writes the following sentence on the board:

    I don't believe that _ _ _ _ _ _ _ _ _ _ _ _.

2. Below the sentence, the teacher writes the following clue words: **institute, vacation, supermarket**.

3. The teacher says, "The mystery word has 12 letters. Listen while I read the sentence. The clue words are **institute**, **vacation**, and **supermarket**. Say them after me. Billy's team won the toss. They can go first. The mystery word is worth ten points."

4. A member of Billy's team asks, "Does the word begin like **vacation**?"

5. The teacher answers, "No, it does not. Jodie's team for nine points."

6. A member of Jodie's team asks, "Does the word end like **vacation**?"

7. The word does end like vacation, so the teacher writes **t-i-o-n** on the last four lines. Jodie's team goes again.

8. A member of Jodie's team asks, "Does the word begin like **institute**?"

9. The teacher says, "No, it does not. Billy's team for eight points."

10. A member of Billy's team asks, "Does the word have a middle like **institute**?"

11. The teacher writes **s-t-i** on the appropriate lines. Billy's team takes another turn and asks, "Does the word begin like **supermarket**?"

12. The teacher write **s-u-p-e-r** on the first five lines. Billy's team confers and triumphantly pronounces **superstition**.

13. The teacher records eight points for Billy's team.

The game continues with more sentences. Some mystery words have only two clue words, one the mystery word begins like and one it ends like. This will seem easy, but it is good for helping students see larger-than-a-syllable chunks. Here are some more examples:

She got a good grade on her _ _ _ _ _ _ _ _ _ _ _. (**compo**sure, confront**ation**, invi**sible**)

The man needed a _ _ _ _ _ _ _ _ _ _ _. (con**fusion**, **trans**port)

The doctor performed an emergency _ _ _ _ _ _ _ _ _. (**op**timistic, confront**ation**, gene**r**ously)

I am going to call for more _ _ _ _ _ _ _ _ _ _ _. (de**form**ity, **in**nocent, convers**ation**)

The answers may be much more apparent to you than they are to students. (In case they are not readily apparent, the mystery words for above are **composition**, **transfusion**, **operation**, and **information**.)

When picking words for Mystery Word Match, be sure that the clue words have the same letters and sounds and that the part of the clue word you want to use is in the same position in the mystery word. Because the sounds of letters in big words change based on where those letters are in the words, students should use *position* in the word as an important clue when they are searching through their word store for words with "the same parts in the same places." If your students enjoy **Mystery Word Match**, you should probably invest in a rhyming dictionary which will let you quickly locate clue words for middle and ending chunks. Sometimes, in the heat of competition, someone occasionally blurts out the answer out of turn. This spoils the game for everyone. Nip this in the bud by making it clear to the students that if anyone says the answer out of turn, the other team automatically gets the points!

Goal Five: Applying Strategies While Reading and Writing

By now, your students should be much better decoders and spellers. Help them to "verbalize" what they do so that they will continue to use these strategies when you are no longer there to remind them. Depending on which goals you worked on, ask them questions and look for responses such as these:

 "Why did we put these words on the wall, practice them, and try to make sure we always spelled them correctly in any writing?"

Students should be able to verbalize that some words aren't spelled logically and that the brain makes things automatic after doing them a certain number of times. This is helpful if you are doing them right but disastrous if you are doing them wrong. **To get wrong things out of the automatic compartment and replace them with correct things, you have to have as much practice as you did getting the wrong things there in the first place.**

Help students realize that there may be other words they have wrong in their automatic spelling compartments. When they notice these words, they need to use some independent strategies for routing them out and replacing them. One of the writers of this book does this by placing tiny sticky notes along the top of the computer with words such as **no one** (which ought to be a compound word like **someone**, **anyone** and **everyone**) and **receive** (which really distracts your attention from writing when you have to repeat the little rhyme every time you need to spell it). When the correct spelling of these words is firmly placed in the automatic compartment, the sticky notes are removed and discarded.

 "Why have we been using the brand names and other words we can spell to help us figure out how to spell and decode new words?"

Help students to verbalize that "that's how your brain works." When it sees something new, it goes looking for other things which are similar to help make sense of the new thing. We call these similar things "patterns." In short words, the major patterns are rhyming words. Thinking of a word that is spelled the same and making the new word rhyme with that word is a quick and efficient decoding strategy. This can help with spelling, too, but there are sometimes two patterns for the same rhyme. **The brain develops a visual checking system by putting familiar words with other words having the same pattern.**

3 *"What can you do when you write a word and you notice that it doesn't look right or you are sure you haven't spelled it correctly?"*

If you write a word and it doesn't look right, you should try writing it with another pattern. If it is really important, you can check your spelling—or which sound-alike word has the right meaning—by looking it up in the dictionary.

4 *"Why have we spent so much time and energy learning to spell the Nifty Thrifty Fifty words quickly and automatically?"*

In English, lots of words are related through their root words, prefixes, and suffixes. The **Nifty Thrifty Fifty** words contain examples of all the common prefixes and suffixes as well as spelling changes needed when endings are added. Being able to spell these words so well means they are readily available in our brains to help us decode and spell thousands of other words.

5 *"What good will it do you to know these things about words if you don't use them while reading and writing?"*

None! We decode and spell words so that we can read and write!

Guess the Covered Word

Finally, summer is here and for some this means taking a trip to the beach! (See directions for **Guess the Covered Word** on page 31.)

Beaches are **popular** recreational spots. Some of the most **spectacular** beaches are found in Hawaii. Florida and California also have miles and miles of white **sandy** beaches. All different kinds of people enjoy a **variety** of activities at the beach. Some people like to **swim** and surf. Others like to sail or **fish**. Children build sand castles and **draw** pictures. The only problem with most beaches on a lovely summer day is all the **tr**░░ you have to drive through to get there and back. Most people, however, think the beach is worth the ░░ it takes to get there.

The above shows what a **Guess the Covered Word** lesson might look like after the teacher has led her students to guess the words *popular, spectacular, sandy, variety, swim, fish,* and *draw.* The word *traffic* is ready for the students to guess and uncover after seeing the beginning sound. The word *hassle* still needs to be guessed and uncovered.

Word Celebration

If you have persevered with your students through the activities they needed from this book, you have devoted a lot of time and energy to equipping them with the strategies and word examples they need to decode and spell the vast majority of the words they will encounter throughout their lives. Perhaps the class should have a **Word Celebration** at the end of the year. The end of the year is a time for celebration and a word party would be very **apropos**. Use some of these ideas:

- Have volunteers bring foods with strange, exotic-sounding names, such as **arugula**, **cannelloni**, and **mousse**.

- Come up with describing words for the aromas and tastes—**tantalizing**, **succulent**, **tangy**, etc.

- Have students describe their summer plans using, of course, vivid describing words.

- Have students write a letter to next year's class, telling them about how wonderful words are and how they will become **Word Wizards**.

Portable Word Wall—August/September

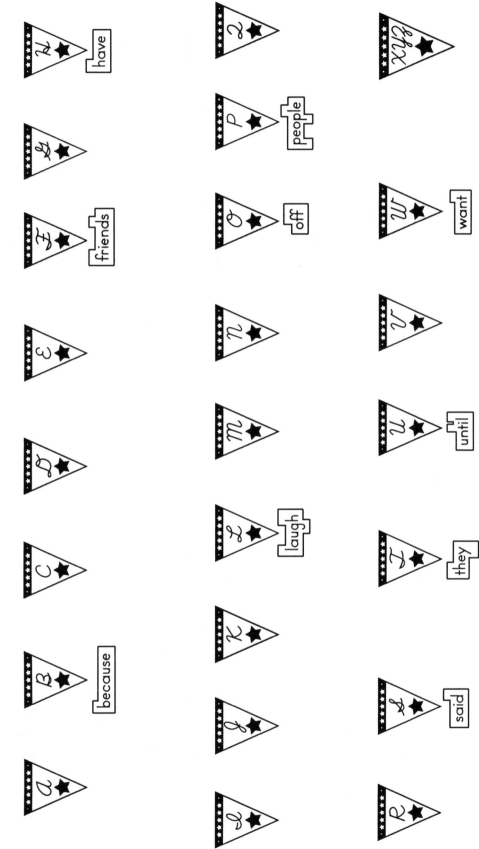

133

Portable Word Wall—October

 again

 because

could

 excited

friends
favorite

 have

  people

off

want
was

 into

said

laugh

until

they
to
too (too much!)
two (#2)

really

© Carson-Dellosa Publ. CD-2405

Portable Word Wall—November

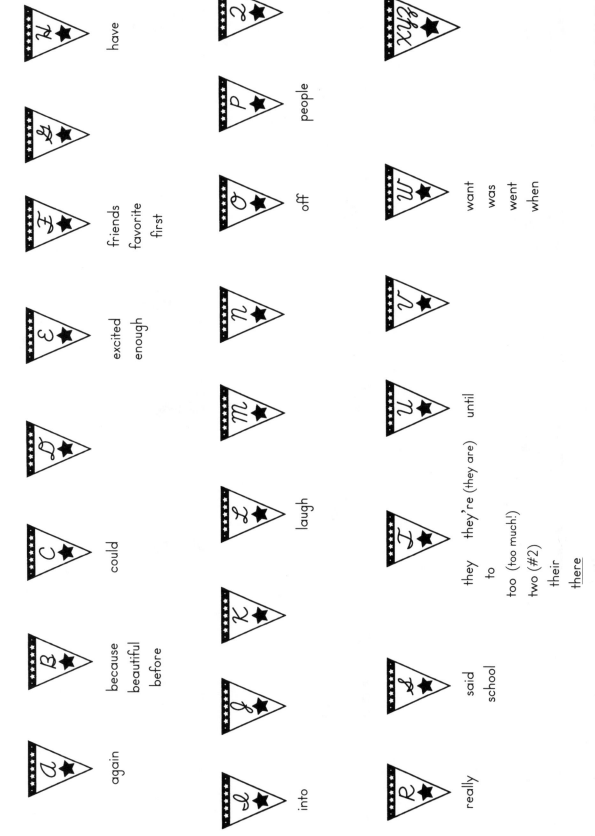

a — again

B — because, beautiful, before

C — could

D

E — excited, enough

F — friends, favorite, first

G

H — have

I — into

J

K

L — laugh

m

n

O — off

P — people

Q

R — really

S — said, school

T — they, they're (they are), to, too (too much!), two (#2), their, there

U — until

V

W — want, was, went, when

yz

135

Portable Word Wall—December

𝒜 ★ again
are

ℬ ★ because
beautiful
before

𝒞 ★ could
can't

𝒟 ★ don't

ℰ ★ excited
enough
everybody
everyone
everything

ℱ ★ friends
favorite
first

𝒢 ★

𝒽 ★ have

𝒾 ★ into

𝒿 ★

𝒦 ★

ℒ ★ laugh

ℳ ★

𝒩 ★

𝒪 ★ off
our

𝒫 ★ people

𝒬 ★

ℛ ★ really
right

𝒮 ★ said
school

𝒯 ★ they   they're (they are)
to
too (too much!)
two (#2)
their
there

𝒰 ★ until

𝒱 ★

𝒲 ★ want
was
went
when
won't
write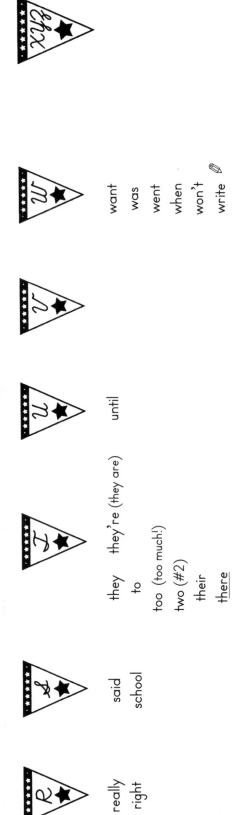

𝓍𝓎𝓏 ★

136

Portable Word Wall—January

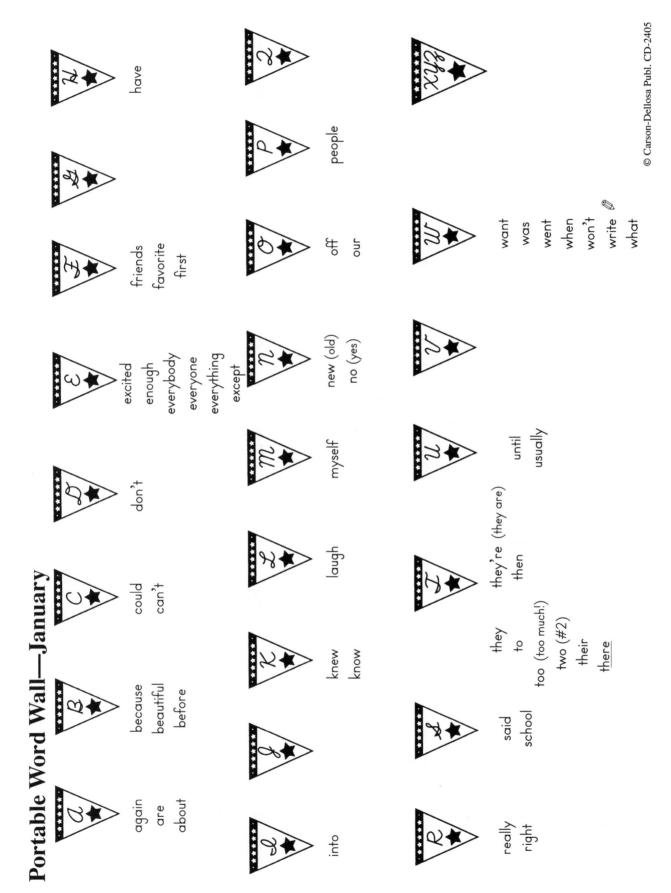

A — again, are, about

B — because, beautiful, before

C — could, can't

D — don't

E — excited, enough, everybody, everyone, everything, except

F — friends, favorite, first

G

H — have

I

J

K — knew, know

L — laugh

M — myself

N — new (old), no (yes)

O — off, our

P — people

Q

R — really, right

S — said, school

T — they, to, too (too much!), two (#2), their, there

U — until, usually

V

W — want, was, went, when, won't, write, what

X Y Z

I (cursive) — into

T (cursive) — they're (they are), then

137

Portable Word Wall—February

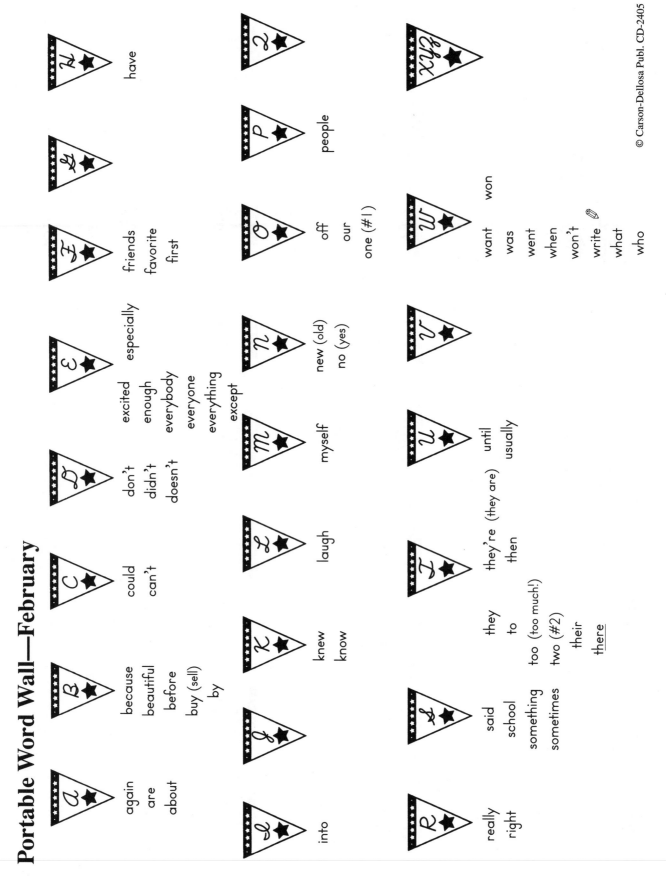

a — again, are, about

b — because, beautiful, before, buy (sell), by

c — could, can't

d — don't, didn't, doesn't

e — excited, enough, everybody, everyone, everything, except, especially

f — friends, favorite, first

g —

h — have

i —

j —

k — knew, know

l — laugh

l — into

m — myself

n — new (old), no (yes)

o — off, our, one (#1)

p — people

q —

r — really, right

s — said, school, something, sometimes

t — they, to, too (too much!), two (#2), their, there, they're (they are), then

u — until, usually

v —

w — want, was, went, when, won't, write, what, who, won

xyz —

138

Portable Word Wall—March

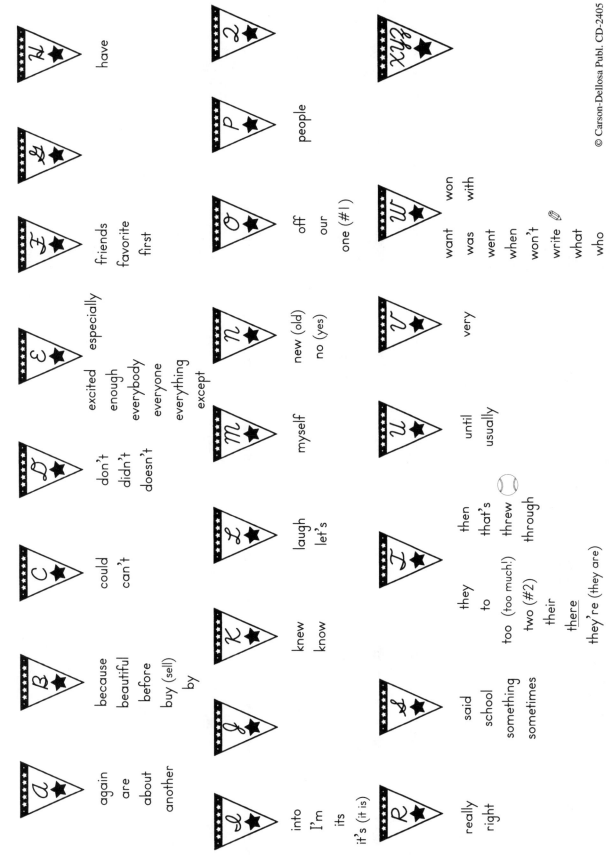

H — have

G

F — friends, favorite, first

E — excited, enough, everybody, everyone, everything, except, especially

D — don't, didn't, doesn't

C — could, can't

B — because, beautiful, before, buy (sell), by

A — again, are, about, another

I — into, I'm, its, it's (it is)

J

K — knew, know

L — laugh, let's

M — myself

N — new (old), no (yes)

O — off, our, one (#1)

P — people

Q

R — really, right

S — said, school, something, sometimes

T — they, to, too (too much!), two (#2), their, there, they're (they are), then, that's, threw, through

U — until, usually

V — very

W — want, was, went, when, won't, write, what, who, won, with

X Y Z

139

Portable Word Wall—April

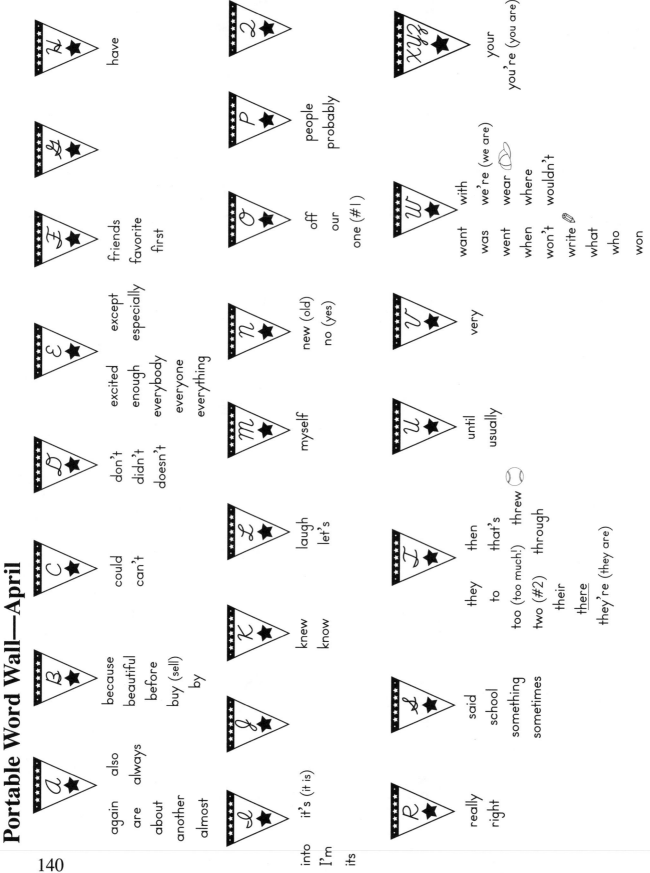

A
- again
- also
- are
- about
- always
- another
- almost

B
- because
- beautiful
- before
- buy (sell)
- by

C
- could
- can't

D
- don't
- didn't
- doesn't

E
- excited
- except
- enough
- especially
- everybody
- everyone
- everything

F
- friends
- favorite
- first

H
- have

I
- into
- it's (it is)
- I'm
- its

J
- just

K
- knew
- know

L
- laugh
- let's

M
- myself

N
- new (old)
- no (yes)

O
- off
- our
- one (#1)

P
- people
- probably

Q
- question

R
- really
- right

S
- said
- school
- something
- sometimes

T
- they
- then
- to
- that's
- too (too much!)
- threw
- two (#2)
- through
- their
- there
- they're (they are)

U
- until
- usually

V
- very

W
- want
- we're (we are)
- was
- wear
- went
- where
- when
- wouldn't
- won't
- write
- what
- who
- won

XYZ
- your
- you're (you are)

140

Portable Word Wall—May/June

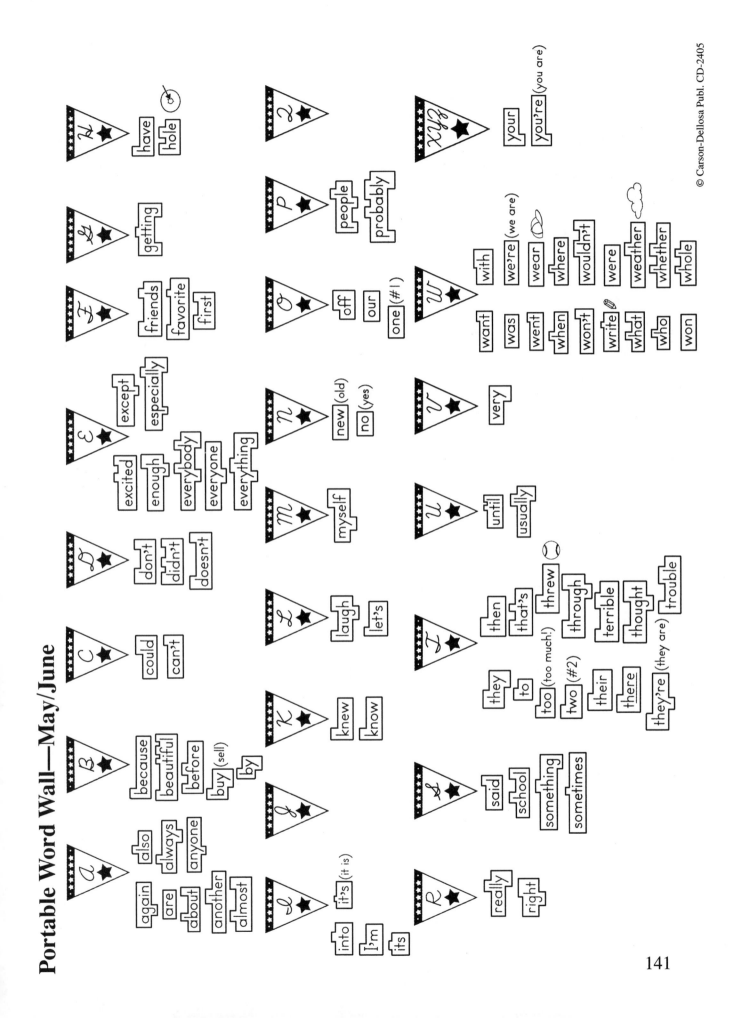

H — have, hole

G — getting

F — friends, favorite, first

E — except, especially, excited, enough, everybody, everyone, everything

D — don't, didn't, doesn't

C — could, can't

B — because, beautiful, before, buy (sell), by

A — again, also, always, anyone, are, about, another, almost

Q — (none)

P — people, probably

O — off, our, one (#1)

N — new (old), no (yes)

M — myself

L — laugh, let's

K — knew, know

J — (none)

I — it's (it is), into, I'm, its

XYZ — your, you're (you are)

W — with, we're (we are), wear, where, wouldn't, were, weather, whether, whole, want, was, went, when, won't, write, what, who, won

V — very

U — until, usually

T — then, that's, threw, through, terrible, thought, trouble, they, to, too (too much!), two (#2), their, there, they're (they are)

S — said, school, something, sometimes

R — really, right

© Carson-Dellosa Publ. CD-2405

141

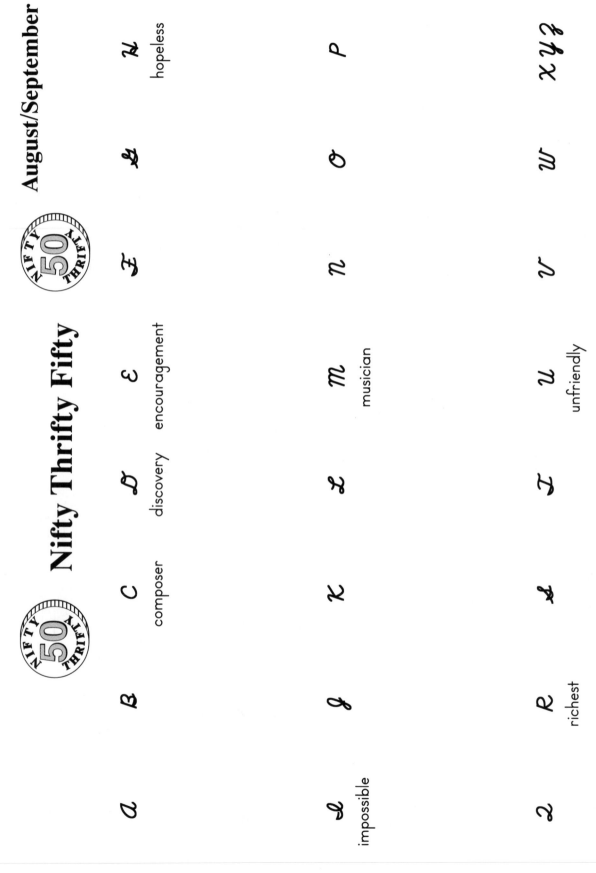

Nifty Thrifty Fifty

 August/September

composer

discovery

encouragement

hopeless

musician

unfriendly

richest

impossible

Nifty Thrifty Fifty

NIFTY 50 THRIFTY   NIFTY 50 THRIFTY

B

C
composer

D
discovery

E
encouragement
expensive

F

G
governor

U
hopeless

g

K

L

M
musician

N

O

P

R
richest

S
submarine

T
transportation

U
unfriendly
unfinished

V

W

X Y Z

a

l
impossible
impression
independence

2

143

Nifty Thrifty Fifty

a

B — beautiful

C — composer, classify, community, communities

D — discovery

E — encouragement, expensive, electricity

F

g

h — hopeless, happiness

I

J — governor

K

L

m — musician

n

O

P — prettier

R — richest

S — submarine

T — transportation

U — unfriendly, unfinished

v

w

X Y Z

i — impossible, impression, independence

z

Nifty Thrifty Fifty

December

a

B
beautiful

C
composer
classify
community
communities
continuous
conversation

D
discovery

E
encouragement
expensive
electricity

F
forgotten

g
governor

H
hopeless
happiness

I
impossible
impression
independence

g

K

L

m
musician

n
nonliving

O

P
prettier

2

R
richest

S
submarine
swimming

T
transportation

U
unfriendly
unfinished
unpleasant

V
valuable

W

X Y Z

Nifty Thrifty Fifty

A

B
beautiful

C
composer
classify
community
communities
continuous
conversation

D
discovery
dishonest

E
encouragement
expensive
electricity

F
forgotten

G
governor

H
hopeless
happiness

I
impossible
impression
independence
illegal
irresponsible

J

K

L

M
musician
misunderstood

N
nonliving

O

P
prettier
performance

Q

R
richest
rearrange
replacement

S
submarine
swimming

T
transportation

U
unfriendly
unfinished
unpleasant

V
valuable

W

X Y Z

Nifty Thrifty Fifty

A

B
beautiful

C
composer
classify
community
communities
continuous
conversation

D
discovery
dishonest
deodorize
different

E
encouragement
expensive
electricity
employee

F
forgotten

G
governor

H
hopeless
happiness

I
impossible
impression
independence
illegal
irresponsible
international
invasion

J
submarine
swimming
signature

K

L

M
musician
misunderstood

N
nonliving

O

P
prettier
performance
prehistoric

R
richest
rearrange
replacement

S
transportation

U
unfriendly
unfinished
unpleasant

V
valuable

W

X Y Z

Z

147

Nifty Thrifty Fifty

A — antifreeze

B — beautiful

C — composer, classify, community, communities, continuous, conversation

D — discovery, dishonest, deodorize, different

E — encouragement, expensive, electricity, employee

F — forgotten, forecast

G — governor

H — hopeless, happiness

I — impossible, impression, independence, illegal, irresponsible, international, invasion

J

K

L

M — musician, misunderstood, midnight

N — nonliving

O — overpower

P — prettier, performance, prehistoric

Q

R — richest, rearrange, replacement

S — submarine, swimming, signature, semifinal, supermarket

T — transportation

U — unfriendly, unfinished, unpleasant, underweight

V — valuable

W

XYZ

148

Making Words Strips—August/September

Lesson One:

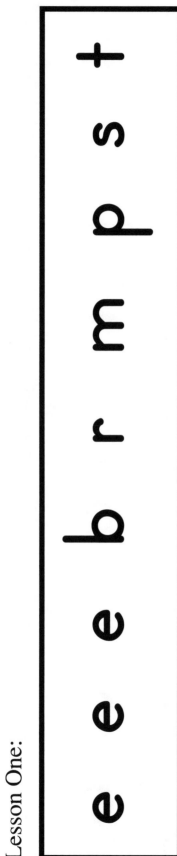

Lesson Two:

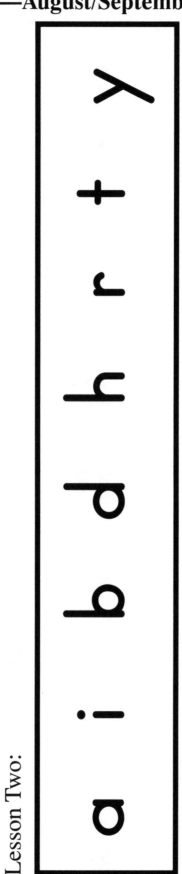

Lesson Three:

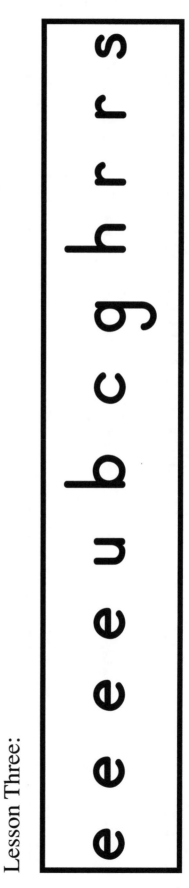

Making Words Strips—October

Lesson One:

e o o b c r t

Lesson Two:

o o u c d h n s t w

Lesson Three:

a o o b f l l s t

Making Words Strips—November

Lesson One:

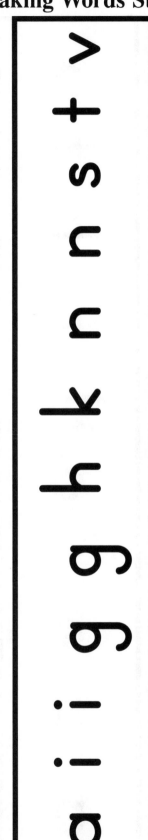

a i i g g h k n n s t v

Lesson Two:

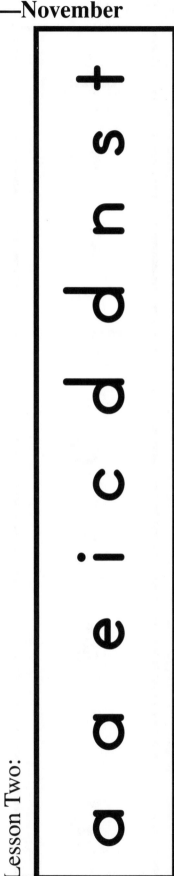

a a e i c d d n s t

Lesson Three:

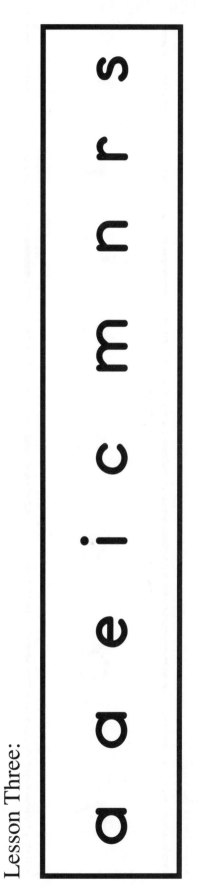

a a e i c m n r s

Making Words Strips—December

Lesson One:

t r l c b e e e a

Lesson Two:

t s r d c o e e a

Lesson Three:

x t r n l o i e a

152

Making Words Strips—January

Lesson One:

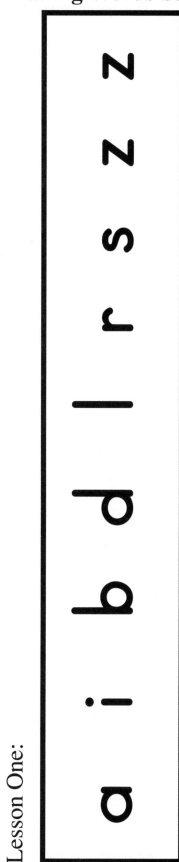

a i b d l l r s z z

Lesson Two:

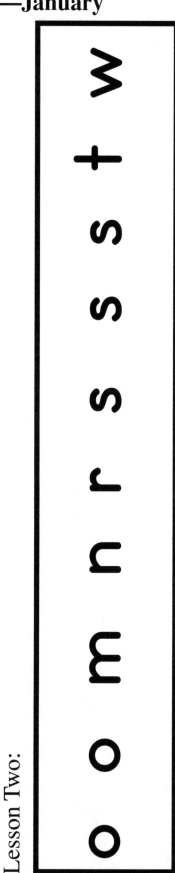

o o m n r s s s t w

Lesson Three:

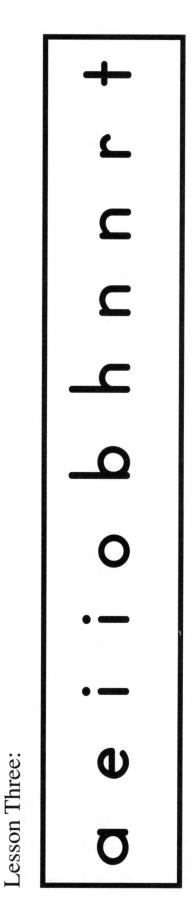

a e i i o b b h h n n r t

Making Words Strips—February

Lesson One:

a e e i l l n n t s v

Lesson Two:

a e u b f r r y

Lesson Three:

e e i d n p r s s t

© Carson-Dellosa Publ. CD-2405

Making Words Strips—March

Lesson One:

a e e n p p r s w

Lesson Two:

a a e b b k l l s t

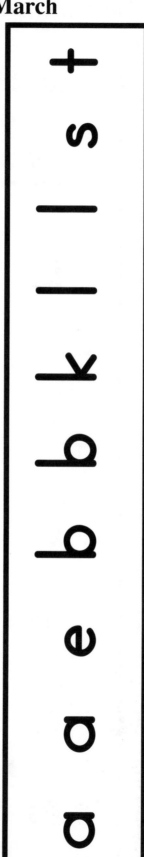

Lesson Three:

a e o u m n n r t t

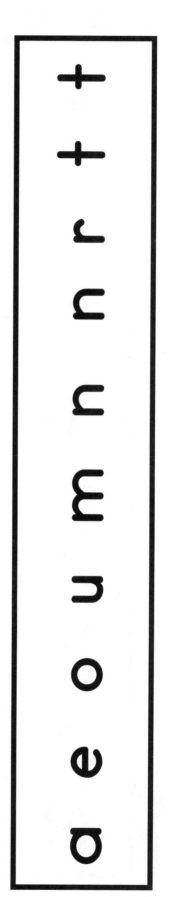

Making Words Strips—April

Lesson One: e e i n n r t t

Lesson Two: e e e o h l n p t

Lesson Three: a a e u n r r s t t

156

Making Words Strips—May/June

Lesson One:

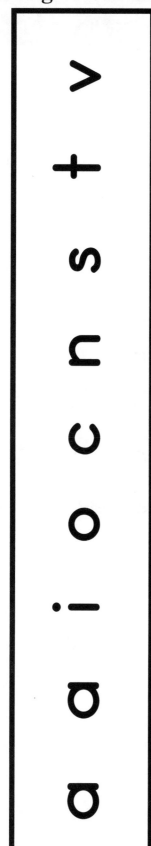

a a i o c n s t v

Lesson Two:

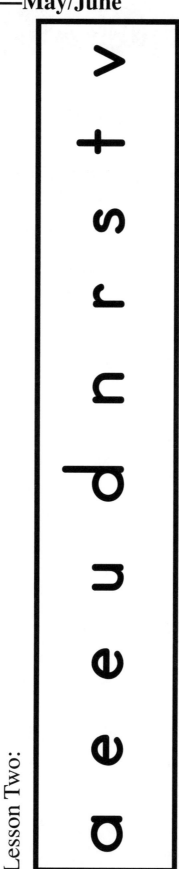

a e e u d n r s t v

Lesson Three:

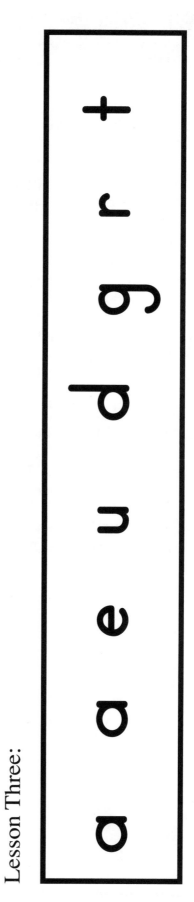

a a e u d g r t

REFERENCES

Adams, M. J. (1990). *Beginning to Read: Thinking and Learning About Print.* Cambridge, MA: MIT Press.

Caine, R.N. & Caine, G. (1991). *Making Connections: Teaching and the Human Brain.* Alexandria, VA: Association for Supervision and Curriculum Development.

Cunningham, P. M. (1991). *Phonics They Use: Words for Reading and Writing.* NY: HarperCollins.

Cunningham, P. M. & Allington, R. L. (1998). *Classrooms That Work: They Can All Read and Write.* 2d ed. NY: Longman.

Cunningham, P. M. & Hall, D. P. (1994). *Making Big Words.* Carthage, IL: Good Apple.

Cunningham, P. M. & Hall, D. P. (1997). *Making More Big Words.* Parsippany, NJ: Good Apple.

Kohfeldt, J., Hall, D.P., & Cunningham, P. M. (1998). "Upper Grades Word Wall Plus." Greensboro, NC: Carson-Dellosa Publishing.

Nagy, W. E. & Anderson, R. C. (1984). How Many Words Are There in Printed School English? *Reading Research Quarterly* 19:304-330.

Treiman, R. (1985). Onsets and Rimes as Units of Spoken Syllables: Evidence from Children. *Journal of Experimental Child Psychology* 39:161-181.